every parent's
family workbook

Triple P Positive Parenting Program®
for every parent

Triple P Positive Parenting Solutions

Carol Markie-Dadds MPsychClin
Matthew R. Sanders PhD
Karen M.T. Turner PhD

Published by
Triple P International Pty Ltd ABN 17 079 825 817
PO Box 1300
Milton QLD 4064
AUSTRALIA

Website: www.triplep.net

First published 2000, reprinted 2007, 2009

Australian English Version
Every Parent's Family Workbook (Edition II)
© Copyright 2013 University of Queensland (Australian English Version)

American English Version
Every Parent's Family Workbook (Edition II)
© Copyright 2013 Triple P International Pty Ltd (American English Version)
Written by Carol Markie-Dadds, Matthew R. Sanders and Karen M.T. Turner

ISBN 978-1-921620-85-0

Layout by Think Aloud Creative Design Agency, Brisbane
Cover design by Tess McCabe, www.tessmccabe.com.au
Text design by Jamtoast, Brisbane
Cartoons by Heck Lindsay
Images: © 2011 Getty Images
Printed in China by Hang Tai Printing Co. Ltd

contents

acknowledgments

The Triple P – Positive Parenting Program® (Triple P) is an initiative of the Parenting and Family Support Centre at The University of Queensland, Australia. Triple P is dedicated to the many parents and children who have participated in the development of the program. Many of the ideas and principles of positive parenting contained in this volume have evolved as a result of the experience and feedback provided by parents and children participating in research and therapy programs. Their assistance is gratefully acknowledged. We also gratefully acknowledge the financial support of Queensland Health, Victorian Department of Human Services, Health Department of Western Australia, the National Health and Medical Research Council of Australia, and the School of Psychology and the Department of Psychiatry at The University of Queensland who have contributed to the evaluation of Triple P over the years.

about the authors

Carol Markie-Dadds is a senior bureaucrat in the Queensland Public Service. Her senior roles have included the provision of strategic advice on future policy directions across a range of ministerial portfolios, implementation of statewide reforms, and regulation of early childhood education and care services. She is committed to evidence-based policy development and bridging the gap between research and practice particularly in the human services portfolios of education, health and child protection. Since 2008, Carol has led the development and implementation of Queensland's strategy for providing all children with access to kindergarten programs, with a focus on increasing the participation of children from vulnerable families. Carol has a Masters degree in Clinical Psychology from The University of Queensland and played a major role in the development of Triple P resources and materials for practitioners and parents. She has previously operated a successful private practice and acted as a consultant to state governments in the implementation of parenting programs in child health services.

Matthew Sanders is a Professor of Clinical Psychology and Director of the Parenting and Family Support Centre at The University of Queensland. As the founder of the Triple P – Positive Parenting Program, Professor Sanders is considered a world leader in the development, implementation, evaluation and dissemination of population-based approaches to parenting and family interventions. Triple P is currently in use in many countries worldwide. Professor Sanders' work has been widely recognized by his peers as reflected by a number of prestigious awards. In 2007, he received the Australian Psychological Society's President's Award for Distinguished Contribution to Psychology and in 2004 he received an International Collaborative Prevention Research Award from the Society for Prevention Research in the US. In 2007 he also received a UniQuest Trailblazer award from the Parenting and Families Special Interest Group in the Association for Behavioural and Cognitive Therapy and in 2008 became a fellow of the New Zealand Psychological Society. Professor Sanders has also won a Distinguished Career Award from the Australian Association for Cognitive and Behaviour Therapy, was named Honorary President of the Canadian Psychological Association (2009), and Queenslander of the Year (2007).

Karen Turner is Deputy Director of the Parenting and Family Support Centre and has a PhD in Psychology from The University of Queensland. She has had a major role in the development of Triple P – Positive Parenting Program resources for practitioners and parents. She has co-authored a range of professional manuals, parent workbooks and tip sheet series, and DVD programs, which are currently being used in over 20 countries. Her clinical and research experience relates to the prevention and treatment of a variety of childhood behavioral and emotional problems, including feeding disorders, pain syndromes and conduct problems. Her research has also focused on the development and evaluation of brief primary care interventions, and the dissemination of these interventions to the professional community. Her work includes ongoing program development, exploring media and interactive online program delivery formats, and making parenting support more accessible for Indigenous families.

introduction

Triple P aims to make parenting easier. This workbook offers suggestions and ideas on positive parenting to help you enjoy being a parent and help your child develop well.

Parenthood can be extremely rewarding, enlightening and enjoyable. It can also be demanding, frustrating and exhausting. Parents have the important role of rearing the next generation, yet most people begin their careers as parents with little preparation, and learn through trial and error. The challenge for all parents is to rear healthy, well-adjusted children in a loving, predictable environment.

There is no one right way to be a parent or caregiver. It is up to each of us to decide what values and skills we would like our children to have and how we will teach them. We also have to develop our own way of dealing with misbehavior. Triple P has been helpful for many parents and may give you some useful ideas to help you meet the challenges of rearing children.

This workbook has been developed as a companion guide for parents completing the Standard Positive Parenting Program (Standard Triple P). The standard program also draws on material from the *Triple P Tip Sheet Series* which covers general parenting and specific issues for infants, toddlers, preschoolers and elementary schoolers. As part of this program, you may also watch segments of *Every Parent's Survival Guide*, a DVD that provides a general overview of positive approaches to parenting with step-by-step explanations and demonstrations of a variety of parenting strategies.

This program has been designed to make sure you have the necessary information and skills needed to practice the strategies introduced in the program as soon as possible. You are encouraged to read the workbook section related to each session prior to meeting with your practitioner. It is also best to make a start on the exercises before your session, if you can. This will allow you to think about the session content before discussing your reactions and questions with your practitioner. The exercises have been designed to further your understanding of the issues raised in each session. They will also help you to use suggested strategies with your family.

We hope that you will find this program useful in undertaking the most important and rewarding job in our community — rearing the next generation.

your first appointment

introduction

At your first appointment, your practitioner will get to know you and find out about your child's behavior and development. You will have a chance to discuss your main concerns about your child and any other concerns you have about your family. This initial interview also provides an opportunity for you to talk about anything you believe might be affecting your child's behavior or development. You will then be introduced to a strategy for keeping track of your child's behavior.

By the end of Session 1, you should be able to:

- Describe your concerns about your child's behavior or development.
- Identify things that may be influencing your child's behavior.
- Start monitoring 1 or 2 of your child's behaviors.

initial interview

For most of this session, you will participate in an intake interview with your practitioner. During this interview, you will be asked about the following kinds of issues:

- Your concerns about your child's behavior and any past attempts you may have made to get help from others.
- Factors that may be influencing your child's behavior such as:
  - your child's development from birth to the present
  - your child's educational history
  - your current family circumstances
  - how family members get on with one another
- How you have been coping in general as a parent and, where applicable, as a couple.
- Medical or health problems that may impact on your child's behavior.
- Your thoughts on why your child behaves the way they do.
- Your expectations about what you would like to get out of participating in this program.

▓ exercise 1 sharing information

As you talk about these things with your practitioner, you may like to note down the main points from the information you discuss.

....

....

....

....

....

keeping track of children's behavior

If you are concerned about some aspect of your child's behavior, it is useful to keep track. Keeping a record is helpful for many reasons.

- It gives you a chance to check out whether what you think about your child's behavior is actually true (for example, does your child disobey every instruction you give?).
- It helps you check your own reactions to your child and see when and why problems happen.
- It helps you see if anything is changing (getting better, worse or staying the same).
- It helps you see when you have reached your goal.

■ exercise 2 choosing what to monitor

List the main concerns you have about your child's behavior (for example tantrums, disobedience, not eating, hurting others, whining). Then define each behavior clearly so that anyone could recognize when it happens.

TARGET BEHAVIOR	DESCRIPTION

With your practitioner, decide which behavior/s to keep track of over the next week. When you have decided, circle the target behavior/s on your list above.

A number of monitoring forms are available for helping you keep track of your child's behavior. Your practitioner will help you choose an appropriate form for monitoring the target behavior/s you have chosen. You can find more information on these monitoring forms over the following pages.

behavior diary

You can keep track using a behavior diary by writing down when and where a problem behavior happened, what happened before (what caused it) and what happened afterwards (how you reacted). This will help you to see:

- patterns in your child's behavior
- how consistently you deal with your child's behavior
- high-risk times or situations
- possible causes
- possible accidental rewards

Use this form for behaviors that happen less than five times a day. For behaviors that happen more often, choose another recording form. You may also like to use this form for 1 or 2 examples each day of a behavior that happens often. An example behavior diary for one day is shown below.

example behavior diary

Instructions: List the problem behavior, when and where it happened and what happened before and after.

Problem behavior: Tantrums   Day: Friday, April 2nd

PROBLEM	WHEN AND WHERE DID IT HAPPEN?	WHAT HAPPENED BEFORE?	WHAT HAPPENED AFTER?	OTHER COMMENTS
Rolling on floor, cyring	7.30 am Family room	Asked to get dressed	Allowed to watch TV a bit longer	
Kicking feet on floor, yelling	8.00 am Family room	Turned TV off told to get dressed	Carried to room helped to dress	I was late leaving house, angry!
Shouting, yelling, stamping feet	10.30 am Supermarket	Not allowed to have new toy	I gave in and bought it	Embarrassed, anything for quiet!
Shouting, hitting fists on floor	12.30 pm Family room	Asked to tidy up toys before lunch	Sent to room Tidied up myself	Screamed for 35 minutes in room
Pouting, crying loudly	6.00 pm Outside	Told to finish game and come to dinner	Smacked, sent to room, no dinner	I felt guilty, TV and gave them ice cream later

tally

Another way to keep track of your child's behavior is to write down how often it happens. To do this, on a tally sheet like the one below, mark off each time the behavior happens during the day.

Use this form for behaviors that happen up to 15 times a day. For behaviors that happen more often, choose another recording form.

example tally

Instructions: Write the day in the first column, then place a mark in the next column each time the behavior happens on that day. Record the total number for each day in the end column.

Behavior: *Swearing*   Starting date: *November 16th*

DAY	1	2	3	4	5	6	7	8	9	10	11	12	13	14	15	TOTAL
Sun	✓	✓	✓	✓	✓	✓	✓	✓	✓							9
Mon	✓	✓	✓	✓	✓	✓	✓	✓	✓	✓	✓					11
Tues	✓	✓	✓	✓	✓	✓	✓	✓								8

product tally

This involves recording the specific outcome of a behavior or series of behaviors (e.g. number of toys broken, chores done, items of clothing left on floor) over a set period of time.

example product tally

Instructions: Write each behavior outcome at the top of a column. Keep track by writing the day in the first column, then place a mark in the relevant column for each behavior outcome you count on that day.

DAY	BEHAVIOR OUTCOMES			
	Make bed	Hang up wet towel	Set dinner table	Dry dinner dishes
Thursday	✓	✓		
Friday	✓	✓		✓
Saturday		✓	✓	✓

duration record

This is a useful form for tracking how long a behavior lasts such as how long an infant cries during the day, or how long a child spends completing their homework or getting ready for school in the morning. Simply time how long each instance of the behavior lasts in seconds, minutes or hours and write this on the chart. At the end of each day, add up the time of each episode to see the total amount of time the behavior lasted. An example duration record is included below.

Use this form when you want to know how long a behavior lasts. For behaviors that come and go quickly or often, use a time sample form, otherwise use a behavior diary or tally.

example duration record

Instructions: Write the day in the first column, then each time the behavior happens, record how long it lasts in seconds, minutes or hours. Record the total amount of time for each day in the end column.

Behavior: Crying after put to bed   Starting date: February 8th

DAY	1	2	3	4	5	6	7	8	9	10	TOTAL
Mon	30 min	20 min									50 min
Tues	10 min	15 min	12 min								37 min
Wed	5 min	15 min	8 min								28 min
Thurs	20 min	10 min	12 min	20 min							62 min

time sample

This form is useful for tracking behaviors that happen more than several times an hour, such as whining, complaining or disobedience. It is best to pick a high-risk time of the day to complete this form. Choose a 2–3 hour time period when the behavior is more likely to occur, such as in the morning before school or in the late afternoon before dinner. Once you have chosen a high-risk time, break this period into smaller time blocks. To complete the form, put a mark in the square if the behavior happened at least once during the time block. Put a dash if the behavior did not happen.

Use this form for behaviors that happen often (more than 15 times per day), behaviors that come and go quickly over a short period of time, or behaviors that do not have a clear beginning and end. Choose another recording form for behaviors that happen less often.

example time sample

Instructions: Choose the time blocks you want to record and write them in the first column. Place a mark in the relevant square if the behavior happens at least once in that time block. Put a dash if the behavior does not happen. Record the total number of marks for each day at the bottom of the column.

Behavior: Whining   Starting date: April 5th

TIME	M	T	W	T	F	S	S	M	T	W	T	F	S	S
3.00–3.30 pm	–	–	–	–	–	–	–							
3.30–4.00 pm	–	–	–	–	–	–	–							
4.00–4.30 pm	–	–	✓	✓	✓	✓	–							
4.30–5.00 pm	–	✓	✓	✓	✓	–	✓							
5.00–5.30 pm	✓	✓	–	–	–	–	–							
5.30–6.00 pm	✓	✓	✓	✓	–	✓	✓							
6.00–6.30 pm	✓	✓	–	✓	–	✓	✓							
6.30–7.00 pm	✓	✓	✓	✓	✓	–	–							
TOTAL	4	5	4	5	3	3	3							

momentary time sample

This form records whether or not a behavior is happening at chosen times. It is useful for long-duration or high-frequency behaviors (e.g. on-task behavior at home or school, sleep, computer use).

example momentary time sample

Instructions: Choose the times you want to record and write them in the first column. Place a mark in the relevant square if the behavior is happening at that moment. Put a dash if the behavior is not happening. Record the total number of marks for each day at the bottom of the column.

Behavior: Playing on computer   Starting date: September 21st

TIME	M	T	W	T	F	S	S	M	T	W	T	F	S	S
Breakfast	✓	✓	✓	✓	✓	✓	✓	✓						
10.00 am						✓	✓							
Lunch						✓	–							
4.00 pm	–	✓	✓	✓	–	✓	✓	–						
Dinner	✓	✓	✓	✓	–	✓	–	✓						
Bedtime	✓	–	–	✓	–	✓	✓	✓						
TOTAL	3	3	3	4	1	6	4	3						

behavior graph

You can put the information you collect on a graph to make it easier to keep track of your child's progress (see below). Keep track like this for a week or so before you start a new parenting plan. Continue to keep track of your child's behavior once you start, to see whether your new plan is working. This will help you notice improvements in your child's behavior and keep you motivated to keep going with new strategies or routines.

example behavior graph

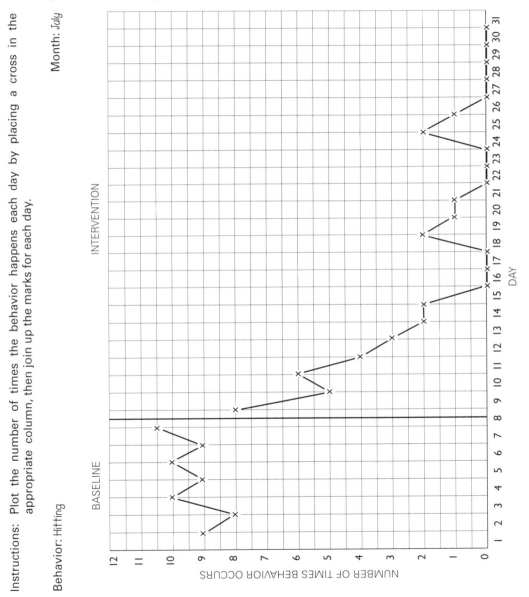

Instructions: Plot the number of times the behavior happens each day by placing a cross in the appropriate column, then join up the marks for each day.

Behavior: Hitting

Month: July

■ exercise 3 keeping track

With your practitioner, choose an appropriate form for keeping track of each target behavior you circled in Exercise 2. Often more than one form will be appropriate, so you will need to decide which form you will find the easiest and most helpful to use. As a reminder, you may like to note down the target behavior/s and the monitoring form/s you have chosen.

TARGET BEHAVIOR	MONITORING FORM/S

conclusion

Today's session has given you a chance to discuss your concerns about your child's behavior and your family. You have been able to share ideas about how you are coping with things right now. You have also looked at some ways of keeping track of your child's behavior.

homework

- Keep track of the target behavior/s for a week using a monitoring form from pages 12–17 (extra copies of these forms can be found in the Worksheets section). After a week, plot your data onto a behavior graph (see page 18).
- Think about the interview with your practitioner. Did you talk about all the things you wanted to? Is there any important information you forgot to talk about? After the session is over, it is common for parents to think of some more things they would like to have said. If this happens, simply note down the key points that were missed. You will be able to talk about this information at the beginning of your next session.

- In preparation for your next session, read through Session 2 in your workbook and, if available, watch *Every Parent's Survival Guide*:
  - Part 2, Causes of Child Behavior Problems, Goals for Change
- As you work through this material, try to note down a few ideas for each of the exercises. You will be able to discuss these ideas at your next appointment.
- To allow for the discussion of assessment findings to happen in Session 2, please make sure you and your partner (where applicable) have completed and returned *Assessment Booklet One* before your next appointment.

what's next?

In Session 2, you will be observed with your child. Your practitioner will outline any special materials or activities you will need for this session, and who should be present.

Make a note of anything you will need:

Your practitioner will talk about what they have learned about your family from the assessment process, and the options for dealing with your concerns. You will also look at some reasons why problem behavior may be occurring and set some goals for change.

For the next appointment, both parents (where applicable) should attend with your child. If you can, bring some toys and activities to keep your child busy during the session.

The next appointment is at home/the clinic at (time) ....

on (day and date) ....

behavior diary

Instructions: List the problem behavior, when and where it happened, and what happened before and after.

Problem behavior: .... Day: ....

PROBLEM	WHEN AND WHERE DID IT HAPPEN?	WHAT HAPPENED BEFORE?	WHAT HAPPENED AFTER?	OTHER COMMENTS

tally

Instructions: Write the day in the first column, then place a mark in the next column each time the behavior happens on that day. Record the total number for each day in the end column.

Behavior: _____   Starting date: _____

DAY	1	2	3	4	5	6	7	8	9	10	11	12	13	14	15	TOTAL

product tally

Instructions: Write each behavior outcome at the top of a column. Keep track by writing the day in the first column, then place a mark in the relevant column for each behavior outcome you count on that day.

DAY	BEHAVIOR OUTCOMES			

duration record

Instructions: Write the day in the first column, then each time the behavior happens, record how long it lasts in seconds, minutes or hours. Record the total amount of time for each day in the end column.

Behavior: ....

Starting date: ....

DAY	1	2	3	4	5	6	7	8	9	10	TOTAL

time sample

Instructions: Choose the time blocks you want to record and write them in the first column. Place a mark in the relevant square if the behavior happens at least once in that time block. Put a dash if the behavior does not happen. Record the total number of marks for each day at the bottom of the column.

Behavior: .... Starting date: ....

TIME	M	T	W	T	F	S	S	M	T	W	T	F	S	S
TOTAL														

momentary time sample

session 1

Instructions: Choose the times you want to record and write them in the first column. Place a mark in the relevant square if the behavior is happening at that moment. Put a dash if the behavior is not happening. Record the total number of marks for each day at the bottom of the column.

Behavior: .... Starting date: ....

TIME	M	T	W	T	F	S	S	M	T	W	T	F	S	S
TOTAL														

behavior graph

Instructions: Plot the number of times the behavior happens each day by placing a cross on the appropriate column, then join up the marks for each day.

Behavior: ....

Month: ....

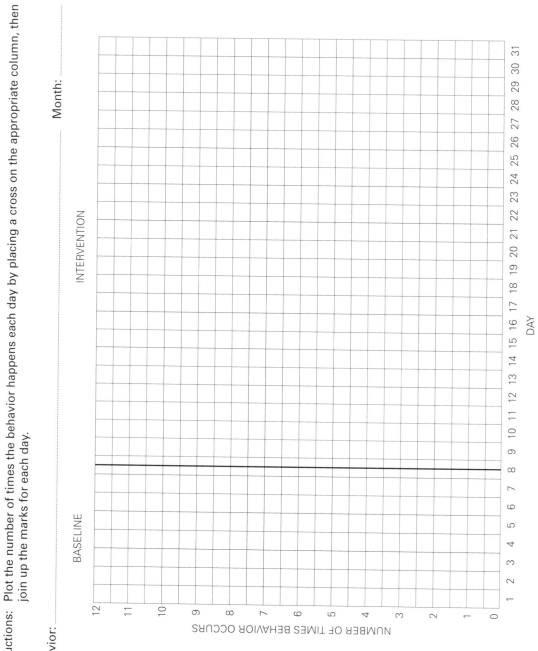

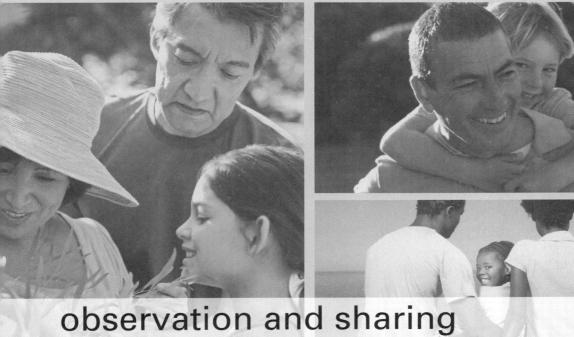

observation and sharing of assessment findings

introduction

During Session 2, your practitioner will observe you and your child doing some different family activities together. Then your practitioner will talk about what they have learned about your family from the assessment process, and discuss some reasons why problem behavior may be occurring. You will also look at some options for dealing with your concerns and set some goals for change in your own and your child's behavior. You will be given an introduction to the aims of Standard Triple P and what the program involves.

By the end of Session 2, you should be able to:

- Describe the nature of your child's behavior problems.
- Identify things that influence your child's behavior.
- Set goals for change in your child's and your own behavior.

observing your family

The best way to understand what is happening in your family is to see it in action. This session will provide an opportunity for your practitioner to meet your child, observe your child's behavior and see how your family interacts.

■ exercise 1 interacting with your family

Your practitioner may ask you to do several different activities together. For this task, act as naturally as possible and do what you would usually do if problem behavior occurs.

results of assessment

■ exercise 2 sharing assessment findings

Your practitioner will discuss with you the findings of each part of the assessment process. You will be asked to talk about your monitoring of your child's behavior. The findings from the initial interview, questionnaires and observation task will also be discussed.

You may like to make some notes about what is discussed.

Interview:

Questionnaires:

Monitoring:

Observation:

why do children behave as they do?

How is it that children from the same family can be so alike in some ways and so different in others? To understand how children's behavior develops, we need to consider many things — their genetic make-up, their health, their family environment and the community in which they live. These all shape the skills, attitudes and abilities children develop and whether they develop behavior problems.

■ **exercise 3 finding causes of child behavior problems**

Children behave in both desirable and undesirable ways for a reason. By understanding these reasons, we can look at what changes we need to make in both our child's and our own behavior to prevent behavior problems. As you read through the next section, place a mark next to those factors that you feel play a role in shaping your child's behavior. You may also like to include some comments in the spaces provided.

genetic make-up

All children inherit a unique genetic make-up from their parents. Along with physical features like the color of their eyes or texture of their hair, children may also inherit other characteristics. For example, children who have problems concentrating or who have a tendency to feel sad or depressed may have inherited a genetic make-up that makes them more likely to have these problems.

Children may also inherit their temperament from their parents. Some children want lots of attention, like to be with others and talk a lot. Some cry and are hard to settle into sleeping and feeding routines. Some are very active and have lots of energy. Others find it hard when things change around them. Some of these characteristics can make children difficult to manage.

Not all difficult babies develop behavior problems as children, and some easy babies do. Children's behavior also depends on how others react to them.

What was your child like as a baby?

- liked to be with people, demanded lots of attention ☐
- easily upset, difficult to settle, distressed by sudden change ☐
- very active, busy, energetic, difficult to control ☐

Comments:

....

....

....

....

health

Sometimes children can seem to be misbehaving and not doing as they are told when actually they may not be hearing what we ask them to do. They may have a hearing problem or ear infection.

If children aren't eating well, they may not have the energy to listen, learn and do as they are told.

We also need to watch for illnesses. Children may act differently and seem more difficult when they are sick.

Do you have any of these concerns about your child?

- hearing problems ☐
- poor diet ☐
- illness ☐

Comments:

....

....

....

....

the family environment

Other things shape the way children grow up. One of the most important things is what happens in the family, and we can control what they learn from us. When trying to understand why children do the things they do, it is helpful to think about what they are learning from what happens around them every day.

accidental rewards for misbehavior

Often there are accidental rewards or hidden pay-offs for misbehavior. An accidental reward can happen if children misbehave and then get something they want. One accidental reward is attention. If we pay attention to misbehavior it is likely to happen again. For example, if you accidentally smile or laugh or spend time reasoning with your child the first time they say a swear word, the extra attention may encourage your child to swear again.

Another example is a material reward. If a child is crying and whining on a shopping trip and we give them a toy just to keep them quiet, this is an accidental reward. We are giving a treat for crying and whining. Accidental rewards can also include activities (such as a parent distracting their child with a game) or food treats (such as cookies, ice-cream or candy) if they are given when a child is misbehaving.

Do any of these accidental rewards happen in your family?

- social attention ☐
- material rewards ☐
- activity rewards ☐
- food rewards ☐

Comments:

....

....

....

....

escalation traps

If children want something and don't get it, they can learn that by escalating (such as getting louder, crying, nagging and pestering) they are more likely to get what they want. For example, your child may ask for a cookie just before dinner. You may say *No* several times, but if your child keeps nagging and gets louder and more demanding, you may fall into the trap of giving them a cookie just to stop the noise. When children escalate like this and get what they want, they learn that it works and they will do it more. What they are learning is that when you don't get what you want, you try harder or get louder and then you get what you want, and you may start to think it is easier just to give in.

In a similar way, parents can learn that if they escalate and get louder, they are more likely to get what they want. For example, if your child doesn't listen the first time you give an instruction, you may say it again and again, and get louder each time. Eventually, you may get angry and make threats or demand that your child does as you ask before you have counted to three. Your child then learns that you are only serious when you yell and count, and may wait until then before they do as you ask. This can make it seem like the only way to get children to listen or do as they are told is to shout and make threats, so this escalation trap is likely to happen again.

Do either of these escalation traps happen in your family?

- child escalates ☐
- parent escalates ☐

Comments:

....

....

....

....

ignoring good behavior

Children can learn to misbehave because others don't pay enough attention when they're behaving well. If good behavior is ignored it is likely to happen less. Children may learn that the only way to get attention is to misbehave.

Do you often fall into this trap?

- ignoring good behavior ☐

Comments:

....

....

....

....

watching others

Children learn by watching what other people do. For example, if children see others get angry and yell and shout and then get their own way, they learn that they can do this to get what they want. If there is a lot of shouting or fighting among adults, children often behave this way too.

Children can pick up other bad habits by watching others. They may learn things like untidiness, swearing, losing their temper, hitting and hurting, drinking and smoking, and how to react when something frightening happens.

Does your child pick up any bad habits from watching others?

- watching others ☐

Comments:

....

....

....

....

giving instructions

The way parents give instructions can influence whether or not children do as they are told. Some common problems include:

- *Too many.* Sometimes we just give too many instructions. Every time we give children an instruction, we give them a chance to not do as they were asked. Too many instructions means a lot of chances for problems to happen.

- *Too few.* Sometimes it may seem that children are misbehaving when they really don't know the right thing to do. They may not have been given clear instructions about what is expected. For example, if we don't give enough instructions about road safety, children may run across a road without looking.
- *Too hard.* We can expect too much and give instructions that are beyond a child's abilities. For example, it may be too hard for a 3-year-old to clean up a very messy room all by themselves.
- *Bad timing.* If we give instructions when a child is busy, such as in the middle of a game or watching a favorite television show, they are more likely to be ignored.
- *Not clear.* Children may not follow instructions that do not clearly tell them what to do — *Denise!* or *Don't be silly* — or instructions that sound like a question — *Would you like to go to bed now?* If we give children a choice, we give them a chance to say *No.*
- *Confusing body language.* Sometimes our body language says something different to our words, such as laughing or smiling while saying *Stop doing that.* Children get confused when this happens and they don't know if we really mean what we are saying. Also, if we give instructions from a distance away, like shouting from another room, children are less likely to do as we say because we are not there to make sure the instruction is followed.

How do you give instructions?

- too many ☐
- too few ☐
- too hard ☐
- bad timing ☐
- not clear ☐
- confusing body language ☐

Comments:

....

....

....

....

emotional messages

Sometimes we say negative things about our children, rather than about the behavior we didn't like. Putting children down or calling them names — *stupid* or *idiot* — and making them feel guilty — *What would Grandma think if she could see you carrying on like this?* — may shame them into doing what we want, but it can also make them angry or resentful, and feel bad about themselves.

Do you give any of these emotional messages?

- name calling or put downs ☐
- guilt-inducing messages ☐

Comments:

....

....

....

....

punishment that does not work

Children can develop behavior problems because of the way parents use punishment or discipline. Here are some reasons why punishment does not work.

- *Punishment threatened but not carried out.* Although threats of punishment may work at first, if we don't do what we say we will, children quickly learn that we are not serious and don't really mean it. Threats of punishment can even serve as a dare, and children may test their parents just to see what happens.
- *Punishment in anger.* Problems can happen when we try to deal with children when we are angry. We run the risk of losing control and hurting the child.
- *Punishment as a crisis response.* Sometimes parents wait until their child's behavior is so bad they can't take it any more before doing something about it. By then they may overreact and be too harsh.
- *Inconsistent punishment.* Sometimes we are not consistent from day to day. One day we follow through with punishment, the next day we just let it go. Problems can also arise when parents and carers disagree about problem behavior and how to deal with it. One person may react one way, the other may react completely differently, or even argue about it in front of the children. Inconsistency makes it hard for children to learn what is expected of them.

Do you have any of these difficulties with discipline?

- punishment threatened but not carried out ☐
- punishment in anger ☐
- punishment as a crisis response ☐
- inconsistent punishment ☐

Comments:

....

....

....

....

parents' beliefs and expectations

Some beliefs are unhelpful and can make parenting difficult. Here are some common unhelpful beliefs.

- *It's just a phase.* If we think misbehavior is just a phase children are going through and will grow out of, it can stop us from dealing with it right away and teaching them how to behave well. This can mean a problem becomes severe and long standing before we do anything about it.
- *They're doing it on purpose.* Sometimes we think children are doing things deliberately, just to upset us. Blaming children like this can make us angry and likely to overreact to misbehavior. It may also stop us from looking at how our own actions can add to the problem.
- *It's all my fault, I'm a bad parent.* Blaming ourselves and thinking we are not good parents only makes us feel bad. This makes it even harder to be patient, calm and consistent with our children.

We can also have unrealistic expectations. It is not realistic to expect children to be perfect. This is likely to lead to disappointment and conflict with our children. Parents can also have unrealistic expectations of themselves. When we aim to do a perfect job, we are setting ourselves up for dissatisfaction and frustration.

Do either of these apply to you?

- unhelpful beliefs ☐
- unrealistic expectations ☐

Comments:

_____

_____

_____

_____

other influences on the family

There are other influences on parents' wellbeing that can make parenting more difficult. Here are some examples:

- *Parents' relationship.* If there are problems between parents, and children see a lot of tension, arguing and fights, it can affect their behavior. Boys may become aggressive and girls may become anxious or depressed.
- *Parents' feelings.* How we feel can also have an effect on how children behave. Feelings, such as anger, depression or anxiety, make us more likely to be irritable and impatient, have unhelpful thoughts, provide less supervision and want to spend less time with our children. We are also less likely to be calm, patient and consistent in how we deal with our children's behavior.
- *Stress.* All parents get stressed and have to deal with problems from time to time, such as moving house, financial problems and work pressures. The problem is that stress can interrupt family routines and children need routine.

Do any of these apply to your family?

- parents' relationship with each other ☐
- parents' feelings ☐
- stress ☐

Comments:

....

....

....

....

influences outside the home

While children learn a lot from what happens in the family, it is not possible for parents to control all influences on their child's behavior. Children are also influenced by others in the community.

friends

Children can be influenced by other children they spend time with. For example, aggressive children often find it hard to make and keep friends. It is likely that these children will interact with and learn from other aggressive children and the problem behavior will continue.

school

Children's success at school can affect how they feel and what they do. For example, a child may have behavior problems because they find school work hard, do not do well and do not get any praise or rewards for their efforts.

media and technology

Children can learn problem behavior, such as swearing or aggression, from watching movies and television programs, reading newspapers and comics, or playing computer games.

Are any of these a concern for your family?

- friends ☐
- school ☐
- media and technology ☐

Comments:

....

....

....

....

All parents can fall into parenting traps at times. You would need to be super-human to rear your child without ever giving an accidental reward or falling into an escalation trap or being inconsistent. Really it is not possible to be a parent without making some mistakes along the way. However, child behavior problems are more likely to occur if you find you are often falling into these parenting traps. So, how often these day-to-day interactions happen is far more important than simply whether or not they happen.

other factors

Are you aware of any other things that could be influencing your child's behavior? If so, you may like to list them in the space below.

....

....

....

....

goals for change

Think about what you would like to change — in yourself and in your child's behavior. Don't try to change too many things at once. Choose 1 or 2 things and set some goals. Keep your goals simple and realistic so you can achieve them. Clear goals can help you focus on what you want to change, help you work towards making those changes, and realize when you have succeeded.

It is up to you as a parent to decide what skills to teach your child, and when your child will be able to learn them. It may be helpful to have in mind the skills that help children learn to be independent and to get along with others.

■ exercise 4 what skills should we encourage in children?

Look at the list below and think about skills you would like to encourage in your child.

How to communicate and get on with others

- expressing their views, ideas and needs appropriately
- asking for help when they need it
- doing as they are told
- playing well with other children
- being aware of the feelings of others
- being aware of how their own actions affect others

How to manage their feelings

- expressing feelings in ways that do not harm others
- controlling hurtful actions and thinking before acting
- developing positive feelings about themselves and others
- accepting rules and limits

How to be independent

- doing things for themselves
- keeping busy without constant adult attention
- being responsible for their own actions

How to solve problems

- showing an interest and curiosity in everyday things
- asking questions and developing ideas
- thinking of alternative solutions to problems
- negotiating and compromising
- making decisions

Comments:

....

....

....

....

■ exercise 5 setting goals for change

When developing your goals for change, consider your child's behavior now. Think of what you would like your child to do more often (such as speak politely, play by themselves without constant adult attention, do as they are told, stay in their own bed all night). Also consider what you would like your child to do less often (such as tantrum, fight, complain during meals, interrupt). It is also important to think about what changes you would like to make yourself. Set yourself some goals. Think about what you would like to do more often (such as stay calm, give clear, direct instructions), and what you would like to do less often (such as use threats, shout instructions from another room).

In the space below, you can list any changes that you would like to see in your child's behavior and your own behavior. Make sure your goals are specific and achievable.

GOALS FOR CHANGE IN YOUR CHILD'S BEHAVIOR	GOALS FOR CHANGE IN YOUR OWN BEHAVIOR

conclusion

Today's session has provided an opportunity for observing you and your child and for sharing the assessment findings. You have looked at some possible causes of your child's behavior and thought about the skills and behaviors you would like to encourage in your child. You have also set some goals for change in both your child's and your own behavior.

homework

- Keep track of your child's behavior by continuing to complete the monitoring form/s you started after Session 1. You can plot this data on your behavior graph.
- In preparation for Session 3, read through Session 3 in your workbook, and, if available, watch *Every Parent's Survival Guide*:
  - Part 1, What is Positive Parenting?
  - Part 3, Helping Children Develop
- As you work through this material, try to note down some ideas for each of the exercises in Session 3 of your workbook. You will be able to discuss these ideas at your next appointment.

what's next?

Session 3 will introduce the principles of positive parenting and practical strategies for:

- Building positive relationships with children.
- Encouraging desirable behavior.
- Teaching children new skills and behaviors.

For the next appointment, both parents (where applicable) should attend without your child if possible. If you are unable to arrange alternative child care for your child, bring some toys and activities to keep your child busy during the session.

The next appointment is at home/the clinic at (time) ....

on (day and date) ....

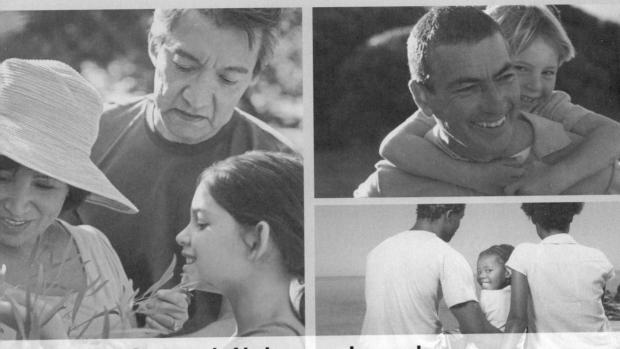

helping children develop

introduction

Encouragement and positive attention help children develop their skills and learn appropriate ways of behaving. Encouraging the behavior you like increases the chances of the behavior happening again. In Session 2, you decided on the behaviors and skills you would like to encourage in your child. In this session, you will be introduced to a number of strategies that can help you promote your child's development by improving your relationship with your child, encouraging your child for good behavior and teaching your child new skills. As you work through the exercises, think about the strategies you would feel most comfortable using with your child.

By the end of Session 3, you should be able to:

- Describe positive parenting and what it involves.
- Use the strategies for developing a positive relationship with your child (quality time, talking with children, and showing affection).
- Use the strategies for encouraging good behavior (praise, attention and choosing age-appropriate, interesting activities for children).
- Use the strategies for teaching children new skills or behaviors (setting a good example, incidental teaching, and ask-say-do).
- Choose two positive parenting strategies to practice and monitor for a week.
- Set up a behavior chart with appropriate rewards for your child.

what is positive parenting?

Positive parenting is an approach to parenting that aims to help children develop and manage children's behavior in a constructive and non-hurtful way. It is based on building good relationships with children and using positive strategies to help children develop. Children who grow up with positive parenting are likely to develop their skills and feel good about themselves. They are also less likely to develop behavior problems. There are five key aspects to positive parenting.

having a safe, interesting environment

Young children need to be safe from danger and have plenty to keep them busy and involved.

Accidents in the home are a leading cause of injury in young children. A good way to prevent accidents is to make your home a safe place. Put dangerous or breakable things out of reach (like medicines, poisons and glass) and keep children out of areas that are not safe. Having a safe home means that you can be more relaxed and your child can explore and keep busy.

An interesting environment has lots of opportunities for children to explore, discover and develop their skills. Having interesting things to do (like drawing, dancing, cooking, building, talking and playing) will help your child develop their language, thinking, attention and independence. If they have plenty to keep them busy they are less likely to get bored or get into trouble.

Children also need to be well-supervised. This means knowing where your child is, who they are with and what they are doing all the time. If you are planning to spend some time away from your child, make sure someone trustworthy is looking after them.

having a positive learning environment

Parents need to be available to their children to help them learn. This does not mean being with your child all the time, but it means being there to help and listen when children want attention. When your child approaches you, stop what you are doing and spend time with them if you can.

You can help your child learn by encouraging them to try things for themselves, and by noticing their good behavior. When you see your child doing something that you like, pay attention. Show your child that you like what they are doing and they will be more likely to do it again.

using assertive discipline

You can let your child be their own person and still expect them to behave themselves. Assertive discipline means managing misbehavior in an acceptable way. You need to make a quick decision and act right away when your child misbehaves, and try to react the same way every time. It is best to stay calm and avoid yelling, name calling, threats or hitting.

When parents use assertive discipline, children learn to be responsible, to become aware of the needs of others, and to develop self-control. Children are also less likely to develop behavior problems if their parents always react the same way.

having realistic expectations

All children are individuals and learn and develop differently. Some learn quickly, others take longer. Learning to use the toilet, put on clothes, help out at home and become more independent are skills different children learn at different stages.

No child will be good all the time and we can't expect them to be. Problems arise when we expect too much or expect children to be perfect (such as polite, happy, neat and helpful all the time). Sometimes children take longer to learn things than we expect, or they have a bad day. It is important that parents and carers understand what children are capable of as they grow and are realistic about when children are ready to learn a new skill.

It is also important for parents to have realistic expectations of themselves. We all want to be good parents, but trying to be a perfect parent will only lead to frustration and disappointment. Be realistic. Every parent makes mistakes. Everyone learns through experience.

taking care of yourself as a parent

Parenting is easier when our own needs are being met. Adults have needs just like children do. We need to feel close to someone and be understood. We need to have time with our friends and time for ourselves, and we need time for activities we enjoy. Being a good parent does not mean that your child should take over your life. If your own needs as an adult are being met, it is much easier to be patient with your child and be available to them. It is also easier to stay calm when you manage misbehavior.

■ exercise 1 what is positive parenting?

Which of these five positive parenting skills do you find easy? Why?

....

....

....

Which of these skills do you find difficult? Why?

....

....

....

What other things are important in helping children develop?

....

....

....

developing good relationships with children

It takes time to form caring family relationships. Here are some ideas to help you develop a strong relationship with your child.

spend time with your child (all ages)

It is a good idea to spend small amounts of quality time with your child often throughout the day. This helps develop a good relationship as it shows your child that you are there for them. Spending small amounts of special time – as little as 1 or 2 minutes – often throughout the day is better than spending longer periods of time together only once in a while.

Special time is when your child comes to you to tell you something, ask a question or do something with you. If you are not busy with something important, stop what you are doing for a while and spend time with them. If you are busy at the time, try to plan some time for your child as soon as you can.

■ exercise 2 ideas for quality time

Quality time is different for all families. Write down some ideas about how you and your child can spend quality time together. Remember quality time is something that can happen every day.

....

....

....

....

talk with your child (all ages)

Talking with your child helps them learn to speak and teaches them how to listen and talk with others. Taking time to talk with them also makes them feel good about themselves. Talk with your child about things they are interested in. Share ideas and show that you are interested in what your child has to say.

exercise 3 things to talk about

List some things that your child is interested in or that you have been doing that you can talk about.

....

....

....

....

show affection (all ages)

Another way of showing you are interested and care for your child is to give them plenty of physical affection. Holding hands, touching, cuddling, kissing, tickling, hugging or just sitting close together can all help children grow up feeling cared for and comfortable with giving and receiving affection from people they are close to and care about. Affection in the first few years of a child's life helps them form secure bonds with their parents.

■ exercise 4 ways to show affection

What kind of physical affection do you and your child both enjoy?

....

....

....

....

encouraging good behavior

Encouraging the behavior you like increases the chance of that behavior happening again. Here are some ideas you can use to encourage your child for behaving well.

praise your child (all ages)

One important way of encouraging good behavior is to praise your child. Notice your child behaving well and praise them for behavior you like. Praise may be just stating your approval — *Good girl* or *Well done, that's great* — or a statement that describes exactly what you like — *Thanks for doing as I asked right away* or *I'm really pleased you tidied up when you finished playing.* Avoid comments that bring up a problem behavior — *It's good to see you two playing nicely for a change and not fighting* or *Thank you for not interrupting.* Descriptive praise is better than general approval for encouraging a particular behavior. Describe exactly what your child did that you liked. Praise works best when you are enthusiastic and mean what you say.

▨ exercise 5 praising your child

Look at your list of goals for things you would like your child to do more often (see page 32). Write down the goal behaviors and some praise statements you could use to encourage these behaviors. Try to be as specific and descriptive as you can.

....

....

....

....

....

....

....

give your child attention (all ages)

There are many ways of giving attention. A smile, wink, nod or just watching are all forms of attention that children enjoy and can be used to encourage behavior you like. These actions add to your praise and show your child how pleased you are with their behavior. You can also use these forms of attention to encourage your child for behaving well in situations where you are unable to praise them, such as when they are in a group of friends and your praise may embarrass them.

▨ exercise 6 ways to give attention

Write down some ways you can give attention to your child.

....

....

....

....

....

....

....

have interesting activities (all ages)

You can encourage your child to play well on their own by making sure they have lots of interesting things to do. Having engaging activities around helps keep children busy, helps them learn, and can stop them getting bored and into trouble. Provide your child with toys and activities, both at home and when you are out. Toys and activities do not have to be expensive to be interesting and fun.

■ exercise 7 thinking of activities children like

Think of some fun new activities for your child. You may like to get some ideas from other parents. You may also be able to borrow some books on children's games from your local library, childcare center, kindergarten or school. List some games and activities for indoors and outdoors.

INDOOR GAMES AND ACTIVITIES	OUTDOOR GAMES AND ACTIVITIES

teaching new skills and behaviors

Growing up involves learning many new and complex skills such as brushing teeth, getting dressed, cleaning up after yourself and strategies for solving problems. Parents need to know how to help their children learn these skills. Some suggestions are given on the following pages.

set a good example (all ages)

We all learn through watching others. To teach your child a new skill or behavior, let your child watch you. Describe what you are doing and let your child copy you. Give some help if necessary, but encourage your child to try again without any help. Make sure you praise and encourage them for trying, and for things they can do on their own.

Don't expect your child to follow house rules if no one else in the family does. For example, you can't expect your child to follow house rules such as *Use a nice voice* if you shout a lot yourself. Set a good example to show your child how to behave.

■ exercise 8 ways to set a good example

From your list of goals for your child's behavior (on page 32), decide if there are any behaviors you can encourage by setting a good example. List them below.

....

....

....

....

use incidental teaching (1–12 years)

When your child comes to you to ask a question, talk to you, get help with a problem or show you something, they are often ready to learn and you have a chance to teach them something new. This is called incidental teaching. Stop what you are doing and pay attention. Just telling your child the answer to a question does not help them learn to think for themselves. Ask questions and try to help your child learn more, figure things out for themselves, and talk more — *What color do you think it is? Yes it's red. What else is red?* Try a hint that will help them solve the problem and when they've solved it, praise them, perhaps by saying back what you wanted them to learn.

This should be fun and enjoyable so don't push the issue. If your child does not respond, just tell them the answer. There will always be other chances to try incidental teaching.

▨ exercise 9 using incidental teaching

There are different types of teaching opportunities that happen often. Think of how you could use incidental teaching in the following situations.

When your child asks you questions, particularly the common *Why?* questions (e.g. *Why is the moon round tonight?*).

....

....

....

....

When your child mispronounces a word (e.g. *sgetti* instead of *spaghetti*).

....

....

....

....

When your child is doing an activity and wants to show you something (e.g. *Look at my drawing!*).

....

....

....

....

When your child is frustrated with an activity and asks for help (e.g. *I can't do this puzzle!*).

....

....

....

....

use ask-say-do (3–12 years)

Ask-say-do is a good way to help your child learn to do things for themselves. It can help you teach new skills such as getting dressed, getting ready for bed, preparing food or doing household chores. When a task is long or hard, break it down into steps and teach your child one step at a time. Follow this process:

ask

Ask your child what the first step is – *What is the first thing we do when we brush our teeth?*

say

If your child does not give you the correct answer, calmly tell them what to do – *First, we put toothpaste on our brush. Now you show me how you put toothpaste on your brush.*

do

If your child has trouble doing what you say, give them as much help as they need to do it for themselves. For example, open the toothpaste tube, put your hands over your child's hands and guide them. Stop helping once the task is started to let your child finish by themselves.

praise cooperation and success

Praise your child for cooperating and for any success at each step. Repeating what your child says or does is a good way of encouraging them – *That's right. We put toothpaste on the brush*, or *Well done! That's great brushing.* As your child learns the new skill, you can use praise less often.

repeat ask-say-do for each step

Repeat this process for each step, such as putting toothpaste on the brush, brushing teeth, rinsing and so on. Provide less help each time your child practices the task.

▨ exercise 10 using ask-say-do

Choose a behavior or skill that you would like your child to learn to do by themselves, such as tying shoelaces, using the bathroom or washing their body. Apply ask-say-do to the first steps in the skill you want to teach. Here is an example of the first step for undressing and dressing:

Behavior or skill: Undressing and dressing

ASK	What is the first thing we do when we get dressed in the morning?
SAY	That's right, we take off our pyjama top
DO	Those buttons are hard to undo, I'll help you undo the first button

Make a start on your ask-say-do routine for the first three steps of your chosen task.

Behavior or skill:

ASK	
SAY	
DO	

ASK	
SAY	
DO	

ASK	
SAY	
DO	

use behavior charts (2–12 years)

Sometimes children need a little extra encouragement to change a behavior, practice a new skill or complete a task. Behavior charts are useful here. They are a helpful strategy that can be used for a few weeks and then phased out. You can put stamps, stars, happy faces, stickers or points on a chart to show your child you like what they have done and you recognize their effort. This can help children feel rewarded for good behavior and trying hard, and makes them feel good about themselves.

You can back up the behavior chart by having a certain number of stamps or stickers earn a reward. Rewards don't have to cost a lot. Some of the best rewards involve activities, such as cooking with you, a family bike ride, special time with Mom or Dad, having a picnic, or something else they think is fun. Other rewards include small treats like a lucky dip, choosing a DVD to watch, choosing dinner, a new book, magazine or small toy. You can work out rewards with your child. Ask what they would like to work for — within limits! Below is an example of a behavior chart used to encourage a child to stay in their bed all night. You will notice that the rewards were made harder to achieve once the goal was being reached easily.

example behavior charts

My happy faces chart for staying in my own bed all night

Day 1	Day 2	Day 3	Day 4	Day 5	Day 6	Day 7
☺ reward	☺ reward		☺	☺ reward	☺	
Day 8	**Day 9**	**Day 10**	**Day 11**	**Day 12**	**Day 13**	**Day 14**
☺ reward	☺	☺	☺		☺	☺ reward

Here are some guidelines for using a behavior chart:

- Get ready all the things you will need. Draw up the chart (see example above). Get the stickers or stamps you want to use, or pens for drawing or recording points on the chart.

- Describe what your child has to do to earn a sticker or stamp on the chart. Be clear and describe exactly what you want your child to do, such as *Talk nicely* rather than *Don't shout*.

- Decide and explain how often your child can earn stickers or stamps.

- Set a goal for the number of stickers or stamps needed to earn a reward. Make it easy at first so your child will definitely get the reward. Aim for at least 2 days of success before the goal becomes harder to achieve. Ask your child to say the goal for earning stickers to be sure they understand.

- Talk about what the reward will be. Agree on practical rewards – not too expensive or difficult to organize.

- Decide on and explain the consequences for breaking a rule or failing to achieve the goal (see Session 4: Managing Misbehavior).

- Praise your child each time they earn a sticker or stamp.

- Give the reward when your child reaches their goal. If your child does not reach their goal, don't criticize, put a black mark or sad face, or take away stickers they have earned.

- When your child is reaching their goal every day, slowly make it harder to get the reward. For example, only give a reward every second day, then only once a week. If your child is working for a weekly reward, you can make the reward a family event for your child to look forward to. Special events that are not possible to organize daily can provide extra motivation.

- Remember this is a short term strategy. Gradually phase out the chart and make rewards less predictable by giving them every now and then. When you stop using the chart and giving rewards, make sure you continue to praise your child for behaving well. Continue to use consequences if problem behavior occurs (see Session 4: Managing Misbehavior).

▨ exercise 11 setting up a behavior chart

Write down the behavior for which you plan to use a chart. Make sure it says exactly what you want your child to do. For example, the target behavior would be *Doing as you are told* rather than *Not being naughty* or *Using nice words* rather than *Not swearing,* or *Sharing* rather than *Not fighting over toys*. Make sure the behavior is clear to your child.

....

....

....

....

....

Think of what to put on the chart (e.g. stickers, stamps, smiley faces, points, stars), and how many will earn a reward. Remember to set easy goals at first so your child is rewarded for their extra effort, then you can slowly make the goals harder to achieve. Ideally your child should earn a reward on the first day of the chart.

....

....

....

....

....

Describe the back-up rewards that your child can earn for a set number of stickers or stamps. Choose rewards that your child will enjoy, such as having a friend over to play, going to the park or choosing their favorite dinner. You can discuss this with your child to get their ideas on what they would like to work for.

....

....

....

....

....

After the next session, you will need to decide what consequences you can apply if your child misbehaves or breaks a rule. Consequences will be discussed in detail in the next session.

List anything you need to get ready before you can start using the chart (e.g. stickers, back-up rewards).

....

....

....

....

....

conclusion

In today's session, the principles of positive parenting and 10 positive parenting strategies were introduced. These included:

- spending time with your child
- talking with your child
- showing affection
- praising your child
- giving your child attention
- having interesting activities
- setting a good example
- using incidental teaching
- using ask-say-do
- using behavior charts

homework

- Choose two strategies to try out with your child. Keep track of how you go by using the monitoring form on page 50. An extra copy of this form is included in the Worksheets section. Note down the two strategies you plan to use over the next week.

....

....

....

- Ask your child what reward they would like to work for on their behavior chart. You can write these rewards on page 47.
- Prepare a behavior chart and get everything ready but don't start using it with your child until after the next session which will provide more information on what consequences to use if misbehavior occurs.

- It is a good idea to keep track of your child's behavior by continuing the monitoring form/s you started after Session 1. You can plot this data on your behavior graph.
- In preparation for Session 4, read through Session 4 in your workbook and, if available, watch *Every Parent's Survival Guide*:
  - Part 4, Managing Misbehavior
- As you work through this material, try to note down some ideas for each of the exercises in Session 4 of your workbook. You will be able to discuss these ideas at your next appointment.

what's next?

Session 4 will look at practical strategies for managing misbehavior and helping children to develop self-control.

For the next appointment, both parents (where applicable) should attend without your child if possible. If you are unable to arrange alternative child care for your child, bring some toys and activities to keep your child busy during the session.

The next appointment is at home/the clinic at (time) ....

on (day and date) ....

strategies for helping children develop

Choose two of the strategies introduced in Session 3 that you would like to practice with your child over the next week. Be as specific as possible (e.g. one goal may be to use descriptive praise with your child at least five times a day). Use the table below to record whether you reached your goals each day. Note what went well and list any problems you had.

GOAL 1:

....

....

....

GOAL 2:

....

....

....

DAY	GOAL 1 Y/N	GOAL 2 Y/N	COMMENTS
1			
2			
3			
4			
5			
6			
7			

managing misbehavior

introduction

All children need to learn to accept limits and to control their disappointment when they do not get what they want. Managing these situations can be challenging for parents, but there are positive and effective ways to help children learn self-control. Children learn self-control when their parents use consequences for misbehavior immediately and consistently, that is, respond right away and the same way every time. Ideas for managing children's problem behavior will be presented in today's session. Think about each of these strategies and how it would work for your family. There will be opportunities for you to practice these strategies to help you decide which ones you would like to use.

By the end of Session 4, you should be able to:

- Set clear ground rules and discuss them with your family.
- Use directed discussion and planned ignoring to deal with mild problems.
- Give clear, calm instructions to your child.
- Back up your instructions with logical consequences, quiet time or time-out.
- Put a behavior chart into practice.

managing misbehavior

There are a number of strategies parents can use to manage difficult behavior. Here are some ideas to help you develop discipline strategies that will help your child deal with frustration and learn to accept limits.

set clear ground rules (3–12 years)

Children need limits to know what is expected of them and how they should behave. A few simple ground rules (4 or 5) can help. Rules should tell children what to do, rather than what not to do. *Walk in the house, Speak in a pleasant voice* and *Keep your hands and feet to yourself* are better rules than *Don't run, Don't shout* and *Don't fight*. Rules work best when they are fair, easy to follow, and you can back them up. Try to involve your child in deciding on family rules.

You may like to call a family meeting and decide on some rules with your family. The main things to remember are:

- have a small number of rules
- rules should be fair
- rules should be easy to follow
- rules should be followed up with consequences
- rules should say what to do rather than what not to do

▓ exercise 1 deciding on ground rules

List 4 or 5 rules that you would like to use in your family.

use directed discussion for rule breaking (3–12 years)

Directed discussion is a useful strategy to help children learn how to follow rules. It is used when a child occasionally forgets or breaks a rule. It involves a quick reminder of the rule and then practicing the right way to behave.

Get your child's attention, tell them the problem and why it is a problem, and get your child to say what they should have done instead. Tell them if they can't remember. Then get them to practice what they should have done. For example, *Carl, you are running in the house, you might break something or hurt yourself. What's our rule about moving in the house?... Yes, walk in the house. Now you show me the right way to move in the house. Go back to the door and start again.*

To make directed discussion even better, get your child to practice the correct behavior twice. If your child does not follow this instruction, use quiet time (see page 58).

■ exercise 2 using directed discussion

Think of a rule that sometimes gets broken in your family or imagine that your child has just broken one of your new rules. Write down what you could say to your child at each step of a directed discussion to teach your child what they should do.

Situation:

....

....

Get your child's attention.

....

....

State the problem briefly, simply and calmly.

....

....

Say why it is a problem.

....

....

Describe or ask your child what they should do.

....

....

Have your child practice what they should do.

....

....

Praise your child for doing the right thing.

....

....

use planned ignoring for minor problems (1–7 years)

Planned ignoring means to deliberately pay no attention to a child when a minor problem behavior happens. It is particularly good to use when a child seems to be misbehaving just to get a reaction or some attention, such as whining for something, making faces, using a silly voice and making rude noises. If these minor problems are ignored, children learn that they no longer get a reaction when they behave this way.

When you ignore a behavior, don't look at or talk to your child. Your child may behave worse at first, to try to get your attention. Just keep ignoring them. If you need to, turn and walk away. Try to stay calm and make sure your body language stays calm. You can take some slow, deep breaths to help you act calm even if you are feeling annoyed or angry. Keep ignoring as long as the problem behavior goes on. As soon as the problem behavior stops and your child behaves well, praise them and give them your attention.

Don't ignore more severe problems such as when your child hurts someone or breaks things. Respond right away (see Exercises 4–7).

◼ exercise 3 using planned ignoring

For which minor problem behaviors could you use planned ignoring?

....

....

....

When do you stop ignoring?

....

....

....

What would stop you from using planned ignoring and how could you deal with this?

....

....

....

give clear, calm instructions (2–12 years)

It is important to give children instructions that are clear and direct, and to make sure the instruction is followed. However, it is not reasonable to always insist on instant obedience. When you want your child to do something, try to let them finish what they are doing (like finishing a drawing or television program), or wait for a break in their activity (like finishing a turn in a game), before giving an instruction. If a problem behavior is occurring, act right away.

When you want your child to do something, follow these steps:

get close and gain your child's attention
Stop what you are doing and move close to your child (within arm's reach). Bend down to their eye level and use your child's name to gain their attention.

tell your child what to do
Use a calm voice and say exactly what you want your child to do – *Heidi, it's time for dinner. Come to the table now please.* If you want your child to stop doing something, be sure to tell them what to do instead – *Theo, stop hitting your brother. Keep your hands to yourself.*

give your child time to cooperate
Wait for about 5 seconds to give your child time to do what you have asked. Stay close and watch your child.

praise cooperation
If your child does as you ask, praise them – *Thank you for doing as I asked.*

repeat your instruction

If your instruction was to start doing something, like getting ready for bed, repeat the instruction once if your child does not cooperate within 5 seconds. If you have asked your child to stop doing something, do not repeat the instruction.

back up your instruction

If your child does not cooperate, back up your instruction with a consequence (see Exercises 5–7).

▨ exercise 4 giving clear, calm instructions

Write down some examples of clear, calm instructions you could use in the following situations. Note how many times you would give the instruction to your child:

It is time for your child's dinner.

....

....

....

....

How many times would you give this instruction? once ☐ twice ☐

Your child is jumping on the sofa.

....

....

....

....

How many times would you give this instruction? once ☐ twice ☐

Your child's toys are thrown all over the floor.

....

....

....

....

How many times would you give this instruction? once ☐ twice ☐

Your child is interrupting your telephone call.

....

....

....

....

How many times would you give this instruction? once ☐ twice ☐

It is time for your child to get ready to go out.

....

....

....

How many times would you give this instruction? once ☐ twice ☐

back up instructions with logical consequences

(2–12 years)

Logical consequences are best used for mild problem behaviors that don't occur too often. If your child does not follow a rule or a clear instruction, then choose a consequence that fits the situation. Take away the activity or toy that is at the center of the problem. Consequences work best if they are brief – 5 to 30 minutes is usually long enough the first time the problem happens. The consequence can be longer if the problem happens again on the same day.

When a problem happens, follow these steps:

take away the activity

Act as soon as the problem happens. Ignore any complaining and don't argue about it with your child. Say why you are taking away the toy or activity – *You are not sharing the puzzle, I'm putting it away for 5 minutes*, or *You won't wear your helmet, so you can put your bike away for 30 minutes*, or *You are still arguing over the television so it's going off for 10 minutes*, or *You are not keeping the sand on the ground, you must stay out of the sand pit now for 5 minutes*.

return the activity

Remember to keep to the agreement. When the time is up, return the activity so your child can practice how to do the right thing. To prevent the same thing happening again, try to help your child solve the problem, such as helping them decide who will have the first turn.

use another consequence if necessary

If a problem happens again after giving the activity back to your child, follow up by removing the activity for a longer period, such as the rest of the day, or use quiet time (see page 58).

Think of some logical consequences for the following situations and make a note of what you would say to your child.

Your child is playing with their drink at the dinner table.

....

....

....

Your child is playing roughly with other children.

....

....

....

Your child is wandering away from you on a walk.

....

....

....

Your child is climbing on the window.

....

....

....

Your child is drawing on the wall.

....

....

....

use quiet time for misbehavior (18 months–10 years)

Quiet time is a short and effective way to help children learn acceptable behavior. When a child misbehaves or does not follow an instruction, quiet time involves having them sit quietly on the edge of the activity for a short time. Quiet time is usually in the same room where the problem happened. Older children can sit on the floor or in a chair, toddlers can be put in their crib or playpen. Short periods in quiet time are more effective than longer ones. One minute of quiet for 2-year-olds, 2 minutes for 3- to 5-year-olds and a maximum of 5 minutes can be used for children aged between 5 and 10 years.

When your child is in quiet time, do not give them any attention. This is a time for them to be quiet, not a time to talk or get attention. Once your child has been quiet for the set time, let them come back to the activity.

It is important that your child knows about quiet time before you start using it. Explain when you will use quiet time and show your child what will happen by taking them through the steps. Explain the rules of quiet time. Check that your child understands they need to be quiet for a set time before they can come out.

When your child misbehaves, follow these steps:

tell your child what to do

Act quickly when you see a problem behavior. Move close to your child, get their attention and tell them exactly what to do – *Daniel, stop pushing your sister now, play gently with her.* Praise your child if they do as you asked.

follow up your instruction with quiet time

If the problem behavior continues or happens again soon, tell your child what they have done wrong – *You have not stopped pushing your sister* – and the consequence – *Now go to quiet time.* Be calm and firm. If necessary, take your child to quiet time. Ignore any complaining and don't argue with them.

remind your child of the rules

As you put your child in quiet time, remind them that they must be quiet for the set time and then they can rejoin the activity. If your child does not sit quietly in quiet time, take them to time-out (see page 61).

after quiet time

When quiet time is over, don't talk about it. Bring your child back and help them find something to do or repeat your original instruction if you had asked your child to start doing something. Praise your child for behaving well as soon as possible after quiet time. If the problem behavior happens again, repeat the quiet time steps.

■ exercise 6 getting ready to use quiet time

What space in your home could be used for quiet time?

....

....

What can you say to your child as you take them to quiet time?

....

....

....

What can you say as you put your child in quiet time?

....

....

....

How long will your child need to be quiet in quiet time?

....

....

When can you talk to your child again?

....

....

What can you say to your child when quiet time is over?

....

....

....

What can you do if your child does not sit quietly in quiet time?

....

....

....

use time-out for serious misbehavior (2–10 years)

Time-out is a positive strategy to follow up quiet time if a child doesn't sit quietly, or for more serious problems like temper outbursts, fighting or hurting others. It is an extremely effective way of helping children learn self-control and acceptable behavior. It also helps parents stay calm instead of shouting at, threatening or spanking a child who has misbehaved. If you become angry, you risk losing your temper and hurting your child. Time-out gives everyone the chance to calm down.

Time-out works like quiet time except your child is moved away from everyone else for a short time. The area you use for time-out is important. It should be safe, with plenty of light and air. Get the area ready before you need to use it. If you use somewhere like a bathroom, make sure it is safe by taking out or locking away anything that might be dangerous or breakable. The area should not have interesting things to do, so if your child's bedroom is full of toys and other interesting activities, consider using somewhere else for time-out.

When your child is in time-out, do not give them any attention, even if they call out. This is a time to calm down and be quiet, not a time to talk or get attention. You may choose to close a door or just keep taking your child back if they come out before time-out is over. Once your child has been quiet for the set time, let them come out. Short periods in time-out are more effective than longer ones. One minute of quiet for 2-year-olds, 2 minutes for 3- to 5-year-olds and a maximum of 5 minutes can be used for children aged between 5 and 10 years.

It is important that your child knows about time-out before you start using it. Explain when you will use time-out and show your child what will happen by taking them through the steps. Explain the rules of time-out. Check that your child understands they need to be quiet for a set time before they can come out.

The guidelines for using time-out are similar to those for quiet time. When serious misbehavior happens, follow these steps:

tell your child what to do

Act quickly when a problem happens. Move close and get your child's attention. Tell them what to stop doing – *Dana, stop screaming now* – and what to do instead – *Use your quiet voice*. Praise your child if they do as you ask.

back up your instruction with time-out

If your child does not stop the misbehavior within 5 seconds, tell them what they have done wrong – *You have not done as I asked* – and the consequence – *Go to time-out now*. Be calm and firm. Ignore any complaining and don't argue with them. If your child refuses to go, take them to the time-out area. You may need to pick them up and carry them.

remind your child of the rules

As you put your child in time-out, remind them that they must be quiet for the set time before they can come out. Leave the door open. If your child does not stay in the room you may choose to close the door or keep calmly taking them back.

ignore misbehavior in time-out

When your child is in time-out, ignore any misbehavior. They may continue to misbehave or tantrum in time-out, such as kicking, screaming or calling out. If you pay attention to this behavior, time-out will not work. Your child will be more likely to misbehave next time and will not learn to calm themselves down. You must be prepared to see it through and stick to the time-out rules. Don't talk to your child or give them any attention until they have been quiet for the set time. Just wait until they have settled and been quiet for the set time and then tell them they can come out.

after time-out

When time-out is over, don't talk about it. Help your child find something to do. Watch for your child behaving well and praise them as soon as you can. If the problem happens again, repeat the time-out routine.

keep track

When you start using time-out, it is important to keep track of how it goes. You may find it helpful to write down each time you use time-out and how long it takes for your child to settle down and be quiet (see the *Diary of Time-Out* on page 71). As your child learns the time-out routine, they should become quiet more quickly and time-out should be needed less often.

common problems with time-out

Parents who have tried a version of time-out may have found that it has not worked for one of the following reasons:

- *The child decides when to come out.* For example, a parent may say — *Amanda, don't speak like that in this house. Go to your room and come out when you're ready to behave yourself.* The child may simply walk into their room and come straight out again.
- *Time-out has been used inconsistently.* Time-out works best when parents use it every time a problem behavior occurs, rather than threatening to use it or using it every now and then.
- *The child comes out of time-out while they are still upset.* This is a problem because the child learns that if they yell loud and long enough they will get out. Getting out of time-out should depend on the child actually being quiet rather than promising to be good or simply being there for a set time. Time-out starts when all noises and misbehavior stop.

▨ exercise 7 getting ready to use time-out

What room or space could you use for time-out in your home?

....

....

....

What can you say to your child as you take them to time-out?

....

....

....

What can you say as you put your child in time-out?

....

....

....

How long will your child need to be quiet in time-out?

....

....

....

When can you talk to your child again?

....

....

....

What can you say to your child when time-out is over?

....

....

....

What can you do if your child refuses to come out when time-out is over?

....

....

....

What can you do if your child makes a mess in the time-out area?

....

....

....

What can you do if your child comes out of time-out before their time is up?

....

....

....

What could happen if you threaten to use time-out with your child?

....

....

....

What could happen if you let your child out of time-out while they are still upset?

....

....

....

developing parenting routines

start routine

The chart on the next page shows how to put together some of these strategies to create a start routine. This routine is useful when you want your child to start doing something such as getting ready for bed, bath or dinner. By following this routine you can break the escalation trap referred to in Session 2. It can help you to stay calm and your child will have less time to escalate if you follow these steps.

example start routine

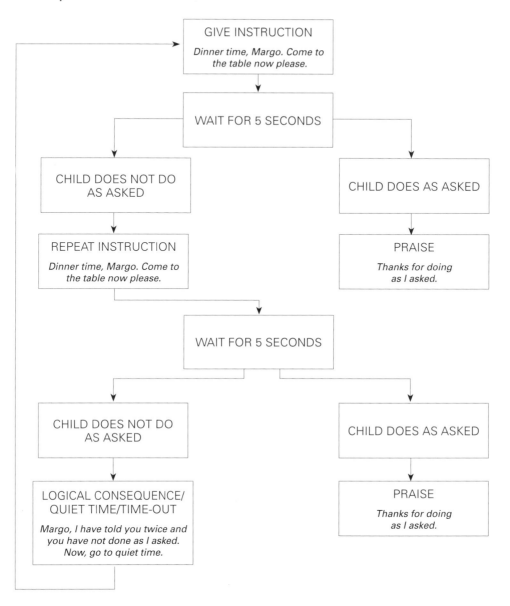

session 4

exercise 8 using the start routine

You will have an opportunity to practice this routine in the session. This practice exercise can help you decide whether this is a strategy you would feel comfortable using with your child. It also gives you a chance to practice the words you would actually say to your child. You can use the space below to make any notes about the start routine.

stop routine

When you want your child to stop a problem behavior, another routine can be helpful. When a problem is happening, only give your child one instruction and no reminder (see below). Example routines for managing fighting, tantrums, whining and interrupting are presented on page 67. Notice the similarities across these four routines.

example stop routine

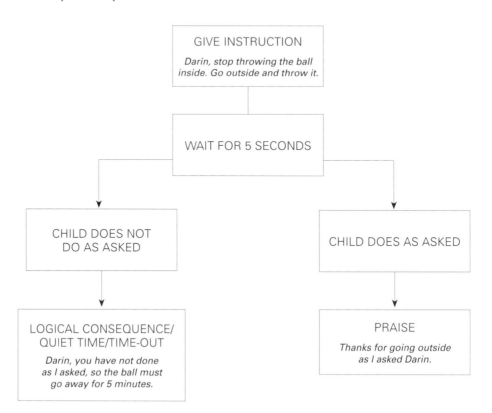

GIVE INSTRUCTION

Darin, stop throwing the ball inside. Go outside and throw it.

WAIT FOR 5 SECONDS

CHILD DOES NOT DO AS ASKED

CHILD DOES AS ASKED

LOGICAL CONSEQUENCE/ QUIET TIME/TIME-OUT

Darin, you have not done as I asked, so the ball must go away for 5 minutes.

PRAISE

Thanks for going outside as I asked Darin.

example stop routines

FIGHTING OR REFUSING TO SHARE	TANTRUMS OR TEMPER OUTBURSTS	WHINING OR COMPLAINING	INTERRUPTING
Get your child's attention. Tell them what to stop doing and what to do instead – *Stop fighting over the game. Take turns please.*	Get your child's attention. Tell them what to stop doing and what to do instead – *Please stop shouting and speak in a nice voice.*	Get your child's attention. Tell them what to stop doing and what to do instead – *Stop whining for an ice cream. Please ask nicely.*	Get your child's attention. Tell them what to stop doing and what to do instead – *Stop interrupting. Say "Excuse me" and wait until I am free.*
Praise your child if they do as you ask.	Praise your child if they do as you ask.	Praise your child if they do as you ask.	If your child does as you ask, when there is a break in your activity, praise your child for waiting and give them your attention.
If the problem continues, tell your child what they have done wrong and the logical consequence – *You are not sharing the game, I'm putting it away for 5 minutes.* Don't argue about it.	If your child does not do as you have asked, tell them what they have done wrong – *You have not done as I asked* – and the consequence – *Now go to time-out.* Don't argue about it. Take them straight to time-out.	If your child does not do as you have asked, tell them what they have done wrong – *You have not asked nicely* – and the logical consequence – *The ice cream goes away for 10 minutes. Try asking nicely later.* Don't argue about it.	If your child does not do as you have asked, tell them what they have done wrong – *You are still interrupting* – and the consequence – *Now go to quiet time.* If necessary, take them to quiet time. Don't argue about it.
If your child complains, use planned ignoring.		If your child complains, use planned ignoring.	If your child does not sit quietly in quiet time, tell them what they have done wrong – *You are not being quiet in quiet time* – and the consequence – *Now you must go to time-out.* Take them straight to time-out.
When the time is up, return the activity. Praise your child for sharing and taking turns. If the problem happens again, repeat the consequence for a longer period or use quiet time.	When your child has been quiet for the set time in time-out, help them find something to do and praise them for behaving well.	When the time is up, if your child has stopped whining, thank them for being quiet and give them a chance to ask nicely. If your child asks nicely, praise them and respond to their request. If the problem happens again, repeat the consequence for a longer period or use quiet time.	When your child has been quiet for the set time in quiet time or time-out, help them find something to do and praise them for behaving well.

■ exercise 9 using the stop routine

Choose a problem behavior and, in the space below, write what you would say or do for each of the main steps in a stop routine.

Problem behavior:

....

Get your child's attention. Tell them what to stop doing and what to do instead.

....

....

Praise your child if they do as you ask.

....

....

If your child does not do as you say, tell them the problem and the consequence, and follow through with the consequence.

....

....

Ignore any complaints. Back up your consequence if needed.

....

....

When the consequence is over, help your child find something to do and praise them for behaving well.

....

....

finalizing your behavior chart

A number of strategies have been introduced for dealing with misbehavior. Think about the behavior chart you planned in Session 3. The final step is to decide on the consequences for when your child does not reach the set goal and for when they actually misbehave.

■ exercise 10 consequences for behavior charts

What can you do if your child fails to reach the set goal?

....

....

....

....

What can you do if your child misbehaves (e.g. throws a tantrum)?

....

....

....

....

conclusion

In today's session, seven strategies for managing children's misbehavior were introduced. These included:

* setting clear ground rules
* using directed discussion for rule breaking
* using planned ignoring for minor problem behavior
* giving clear, calm instructions
* backing up instructions with logical consequences
* using quiet time for misbehavior
* using time-out for serious misbehavior

You were also introduced to the start routine and stop routine which include some of these strategies. You have also had a chance to finalize your behavior chart.

homework

- Decide on 4 or 5 ground rules and discuss them with your family.
- Choose the strategies that you would like to try out with your child. If you choose to use time-out, keep track of how you go. Use the monitoring form on page 71. An extra copy of this form is provided in the Worksheets section. Choose a time to talk to your child about your new strategies before you use them. If possible, start using your new strategies on a day when you are likely to be at home and when you are not in a hurry or have lots of things you have to get done. Note down the strategies you plan to use over the next week.

....

....

....

....

- Start using the behavior chart you designed in Session 3, with the consequences you have just decided on.
- It is a good idea to keep track of your child's progress by continuing the monitoring form you started in Session 1. Putting this information on a behavior graph can help you see what is changing as you start to use the strategies introduced this week and in Session 3.
- In preparation for the next session, read through Session 5 of your workbook.

what's next?

Next are some practice sessions that may be conducted in your home or the clinic. These practice sessions give you the chance to get some support and feedback in using the positive parenting strategies introduced in Sessions 3 and 4 with your child. Work with your practitioner to set some goals for the practice task. Note your goals in Exercise 1 on page 74. During these practice sessions, you will be prompted to track your use of the strategies, think about what you're doing well and what you could improve on, and set goals for change.

For the next appointment, both parents (where applicable) should be available with your child.

The next appointment is at home/the clinic at (time) ....

on (day and date) ....

diary of time-out

Instructions: Make a note of the day, the problem behavior, when and where it occurred, and the total length of time your child was in time-out.

Set time for time-out: 2 minutes ☐   3 minutes ☐   4 minutes ☐   5 minutes ☐

DAY	PROBLEM	WHEN AND WHERE IT HAPPENED	LENGTH OF TIME-OUT

using positive parenting strategies 1

introduction

Today's practice session may be held in your home or at the clinic. Remember to review your goals for this session before your practitioner arrives. Please read over the positive parenting strategies introduced in Sessions 3 and 4. When your practitioner arrives, they will ask you your goals for the session and then set up a practice task where you spend 15–20 minutes with your child. After this practice, you will review your use of the positive parenting strategies and set some goals for the next few days.

By the end of Session 5, you should be able to:

- Use positive parenting strategies with your child.
- Monitor your use of positive parenting strategies.
- Notice what you are doing well in using positive parenting strategies and what you could improve on.
- Set specific goals for further practice.

getting started

To help the practice session run as smoothly as possible, please follow these guidelines if the session is in your home:

- Turn the television, DVD and computer games off during the practice session.
- Keep incoming telephone calls brief and do not make any outgoing calls.
- Keep all family members in the same area during the practice task so your practitioner can easily see and hear what is happening.
- Do not speak to your practitioner during the practice task.

practice task

Think about how you can set up the practice task to increase the likelihood that you will achieve your goals. For example, if your goal is to use praise and incidental teaching to encourage your child to play on their own, spend part of the practice session with your child and then part of the time doing your own thing. This will give you more chances to praise your child for playing by themselves. If your goal is to give clear, calm instructions, plan your instructions before the practice task. For example, spend some time playing with your child and then ask them to clean up or wash their hands to change activities or have a snack. This would give you a chance to practice giving instructions and backing them up with consequences.

▨ exercise 1 setting goals for the practice task

List your goals for today's practice task — be as specific as you can (e.g. use descriptive praise three times; give clear, calm instructions; back up instructions with consequences, quiet time or time-out).

....

....

....

....

▨ exercise 2 keeping track of what you do

During the practice task, you may like to use the checklists on the following pages to remind yourself of the steps for dealing with some common problem behaviors or a target behavior you have discussed with your practitioner. You can also refer to them after the practice task to see how well you went. These checklists can help you work out which steps you follow well and any steps you may have forgotten or need to practice. This can help when you are setting goals for change. You can also use the checklists at other times if any of these problems happen. Extra copies of these checklists are included in the Worksheets section.

checklist for managing interrupting

Instructions: When your child has interrupted a conversation or activity, write Yes, No or NA (Not Applicable) for each of the steps below.

STEPS TO FOLLOW	DAY						
	STEPS COMPLETED?						
1. Get your child's attention.							
2. Tell your child what to stop doing and what to do instead — *Stop interrupting. Say "Excuse me" and wait until I am free.*							
3. If your child does as you ask, when there is a break in your activity, praise them for waiting and give them your attention.							
4. If your child does not do as you have asked, tell them what they have done wrong — *You are still interrupting* — and the consequence — *Now go to quiet time.* If necessary, take them to quiet time. Don't argue about it.							
5. If your child does not sit quietly in quiet time, tell them what they have done wrong — *You are not being quiet in quiet time* — and the consequence — *Now you must go to time-out.* Take them straight to time-out.							
6. When your child has been quiet for the set time in quiet time or time-out, help them find something to do.							
7. As soon as possible, praise your child for behaving well.							
NUMBER OF STEPS COMPLETED:							

checklist for managing fighting or not sharing

Instructions: When fighting or not sharing or taking turns with other children happens, record Yes, No or NA (Not Applicable) for each of the steps below.

STEPS TO FOLLOW	DAY							
	STEPS COMPLETED?							
1. Get your child's attention.								
2. Tell your child what to stop doing and what to do instead — *Stop fighting over the game. Take turns please.*								
3. Praise the children if they do as you ask.								
4. If the problem continues, tell your child what they have done wrong and the logical consequence — *You are not taking turns, I'm putting the game away for 5 minutes.* Don't argue about it.								
5. If your child complains, use planned ignoring.								
6. When the time is up, return the activity.								
7. As soon as possible, praise the children for sharing and taking turns.								
8. If the problem happens again, repeat the logical consequence for a longer time or use quiet time.								
NUMBER OF STEPS COMPLETED:								

session 5

checklist for managing aggression

Instructions: When aggression happens, record Yes, No or NA (Not Applicable) for each of the steps below.

STEPS TO FOLLOW	DAY — STEPS COMPLETED?						
1. Get your child's attention.							
2. Tell your child what to stop doing and what to do instead — *Stop hitting. Keep your hands to yourself.*							
3. Praise your child if they do as you ask.							
4. If your child does not do as you have asked, tell them what they have done wrong — *You are still hitting* — and the consequence — *Now go to quiet time.* If necessary, take them to quiet time. Don't argue about it.							
5. If your child does not sit quietly in quiet time, tell them what they have done wrong — *You are not being quiet in quiet time* — and the consequence — *Now you must go to time-out.* Take them straight to time-out.							
6. When your child has been quiet for the set time in quiet time or time-out, help them find something to do.							
7. As soon as possible, praise your child for behaving well.							
NUMBER OF STEPS COMPLETED:							

checklist for managing temper outbursts

Instructions: When temper outbursts (e.g. screaming, crying or stamping feet) happen, record Yes, No or NA (Not Applicable) for each of the steps below.

STEPS TO FOLLOW	DAY						
	STEPS COMPLETED?						
EITHER A) Use planned ignoring for toddlers under 2 years old. OR B) Get your child's attention as best you can and follow the steps below:							
1. Tell your child what to stop doing and what to do instead — *Stop screaming right now. Use a nice voice.*							
2. Praise your child if they do as you ask.							
3. If your child does not do as you have asked, tell them what they have done wrong — *You have not done as I asked* — and the consequence — *Now go to time-out.* Don't argue about it. Take them straight to time-out.							
4. When your child has been quiet for the set time in time-out, help them find something to do.							
5. As soon as possible, praise your child for behaving well.							
NUMBER OF STEPS COMPLETED:							

checklist for managing whining

Instructions: When whining for something happens, record Yes, No or NA (Not Applicable) for each of the steps below.

STEPS TO FOLLOW	DAY							
	STEPS COMPLETED?							
1. Get your child's attention.								
2. Tell your child what to stop doing and what to do instead — *Stop whining for a piece of cake. Please ask nicely.*								
3. Praise your child if they do as you ask.								
4. If your child does not do as you have asked, tell them what they have done wrong — *You have not asked nicely* — and the consequence — *The cake goes away for 10 minutes.* Try again then. Don't argue about it.								
5. If your child complains, use planned ignoring.								
6. When the time is up, if your child has stopped whining, praise them for being quiet and give them a chance to ask nicely for what they want.								
7. If your child asks nicely, praise them for asking nicely and respond to their request.								
8. If the problem happens again, repeat the logical consequence for a longer time or use quiet time.								
NUMBER OF STEPS COMPLETED:								

session 5

checklist for managing problem behavior

Instructions: When problem behavior happens, record Yes, No or NA (Not Applicable) for each of the steps below.

STEPS TO FOLLOW	DAY						
	STEPS COMPLETED?						
NUMBER OF STEPS COMPLETED:							

session 5

■ exercise 3 reviewing the practice task

What do you feel *you* did well during the practice task? Refer to the goals you set in Exercise 1. Which goals did you achieve?

....

....

....

....

....

....

....

What do you feel *you* could have done differently to improve on this practice task? Think about the goals you set in Exercise 1. Was there a goal you did not reach?

....

....

....

....

....

....

....

other issues

Use the space below to make notes about any other issues discussed in the session.

....

....

....

....

....

conclusion

In today's session, you had a chance to use the positive parenting strategies in front of your practitioner. You were also able to refine your parenting plans by monitoring your behavior, noticing what you're doing well and what you'd like to do differently, and setting goals for change.

homework

- Make a note of the homework tasks you would like to complete before your next session.
- Skills to practice:

....

....

....

....

- Other homework tasks and suggested reading:

....

....

....

....

- It is a good idea to continue to keep track of your child's behavior and plot this data on your behavior graph. Stop monitoring once the behavior has reached a level you are happy with for 5 days. You can then start keeping track of another behavior if you like.
- Before your next practice session, set goals for the practice task and note them down in Exercise 1 on page 86.

what's next?

The next session will give you another chance to track your use of the positive parenting strategies. You will be able to to set some specific goals for the practice task, and then work out what you are doing well and what you could improve on, and set further goals for change.

For the next appointment, both parents (where applicable) should be available with your child.

The next appointment is at home/the clinic at (time) ....

on (day and date) ....

using positive parenting strategies 2

introduction

This practice session may be held in your home or at the clinic, and gives you another chance to practice using the positive parenting strategies with support from your practitioner. Remember to set your goals for today's session before your practitioner arrives. Aim to build on what happened in your last practice session. It is likely that your goals for today will be related to the skills you have been practicing over the last few days. Again, you will be prompted to track how you go, think about what you are doing well and what you would like to do differently, and set further goals for change.

By the end of Session 6, you should be able to:

- Use positive parenting strategies with your child.
- Monitor your use of positive parenting strategies.
- Notice what you are doing well in using positive parenting strategies and what you could improve on.
- Set specific goals for further practice.

getting started

To help the practice session run as smoothly as possible, please follow these guidelines if the session is in your home:

- Turn the television, DVD and computer games off during the practice session.
- Keep incoming telephone calls brief and do not make any outgoing calls.
- Keep all family members in the same area during the practice task so your practitioner can easily see and hear what is happening.
- Do not speak to your practitioner during the practice task.

practice task

■ exercise 1 setting goals for the practice task

List your goals for today's practice task — be as specific as you can.

....

....

....

....

■ exercise 2 keeping track of what you do

During the practice task, you may like to use the checklists on the following pages to remind yourself of the steps for dealing with some common problem behaviors or a target behavior you have discussed with your practitioner. You can also refer to them after the practice task to see how well you went. These checklists can help you work out which steps you follow well and any steps you may have forgotten or need to practice. This can help when you are setting goals for change. You can also use the checklists at other times if any of these problems happen. Extra copies of these checklists are included in the Worksheets section.

checklist for managing interrupting

Instructions: When your child has interrupted a conversation or activity, write Yes, No or NA (Not Applicable) for each of the steps below.

	DAY						
STEPS TO FOLLOW	**STEPS COMPLETED?**						
1. Get your child's attention.							
2. Tell your child what to stop doing and what to do instead — *Stop interrupting. Say "Excuse me" and wait until I am free.*							
3. If your child does as you ask, when there is a break in your activity, praise them for waiting and give them your attention.							
4. If your child does not do as you have asked, tell them what they have done wrong — *You are still interrupting* — and the consequence — *Now go to quiet time.* If necessary, take them to quiet time. Don't argue about it.							
5. If your child does not sit quietly in quiet time, tell them what they have done wrong — *You are not being quiet in quiet time* — and the consequence — *Now you must go to time-out.* Take them straight to time-out.							
6. When your child has been quiet for the set time in quiet time or time-out, help them find something to do.							
7. As soon as possible, praise your child for behaving well.							
NUMBER OF STEPS COMPLETED:							

session 6

checklist for managing fighting or not sharing

Instructions: When fighting or not sharing or taking turns with other children happens, record Yes, No or NA (Not Applicable) for each of the steps below.

STEPS TO FOLLOW	DAY						
	STEPS COMPLETED?						
1. Get your child's attention.							
2. Tell your child what to stop doing and what to do instead — *Stop fighting over the game. Take turns please.*							
3. Praise the children if they do as you ask.							
4. If the problem continues, tell your child what they have done wrong and the logical consequence — *You are not taking turns, I'm putting the game away for 5 minutes.* Don't argue about it.							
5. If your child complains, use planned ignoring.							
6. When the time is up, return the activity.							
7. As soon as possible, praise the children for sharing and taking turns.							
8. If the problem happens again, repeat the logical consequence for a longer time or use quiet time.							
NUMBER OF STEPS COMPLETED:							

session 6

checklist for managing aggression

Instructions: When aggression happens, record Yes, No or NA (Not Applicable) for each of the steps below.

STEPS TO FOLLOW	DAY						
	STEPS COMPLETED?						
1. Get your child's attention.							
2. Tell your child what to stop doing and what to do instead — *Stop hitting. Keep your hands to yourself.*							
3. Praise your child if they do as you ask.							
4. If your child does not do as you have asked, tell them what they have done wrong — *You are still hitting* — and the consequence — *Now go to quiet time.* If necessary, take them to quiet time. Don't argue about it.							
5. If your child does not sit quietly in quiet time, tell them what they have done wrong — *You are not being quiet in quiet time* — and the consequence — *Now you must go to time-out.* Take them straight to time-out.							
6. When your child has been quiet for the set time in quiet time or time-out, help them find something to do.							
7. As soon as possible, praise your child for behaving well.							
NUMBER OF STEPS COMPLETED:							

session 6

checklist for managing temper outbursts

Instructions: When temper outbursts (e.g. screaming, crying or stamping feet) happen, record Yes, No or NA (Not Applicable) for each of the steps below.

STEPS TO FOLLOW	DAY — STEPS COMPLETED?						
EITHER A) Use planned ignoring for toddlers under 2 years old. OR B) Get your child's attention as best you can and follow the steps below:							
1. Tell your child what to stop doing and what to do instead — *Stop screaming right now. Use a nice voice.*							
2. Praise your child if they do as you ask.							
3. If your child does not do as you have asked, tell them what they have done wrong — *You have not done as I asked* — and the consequence — *Now go to time-out.* Don't argue about it. Take them straight to time-out.							
4. When your child has been quiet for the set time in time-out, help them find something to do.							
5. As soon as possible, praise your child for behaving well.							
NUMBER OF STEPS COMPLETED:							

checklist for managing whining

Instructions: When whining for something happens, record Yes, No or NA (Not Applicable) for each of the steps below.

STEPS TO FOLLOW	DAY						
	STEPS COMPLETED?						
1. Get your child's attention.							
2. Tell your child what to stop doing and what to do instead — *Stop whining for a piece of cake. Please ask nicely.*							
3. Praise your child if they do as you ask.							
4. If your child does not do as you have asked, tell them what they have done wrong — *You have not asked nicely* — and the consequence — *The cake goes away for 10 minutes.* Try again then. Don't argue about it.							
5. If your child complains, use planned ignoring.							
6. When the time is up, if your child has stopped whining, praise them for being quiet and give them a chance to ask nicely for what they want.							
7. If your child asks nicely, praise them for asking nicely and respond to their request.							
8. If the problem happens again, repeat the logical consequence for a longer time or use quiet time.							
NUMBER OF STEPS COMPLETED:							

session 6

checklist for managing problem behavior

Instructions: When problem behavior happens, record Yes, No or NA (Not Applicable) for each of the steps below.

	DAY							
STEPS TO FOLLOW	STEPS COMPLETED?							
NUMBER OF STEPS COMPLETED:								

session 6

■ exercise 3 reviewing the practice task

What do you feel *you* did well during the practice task? Refer to the goals you set in Exercise 1. Which goals did you achieve?

....

....

....

....

....

....

....

What do you feel *you* could have done differently to improve on this practice task? Think about the goals you set in Exercise 1. Was there a goal you did not reach?

....

....

....

....

....

....

....

....

....

other issues

You may like to use the space below to make notes about any other issues discussed in the session.

....

....

....

....

....

....

conclusion

In today's session, you had another chance to use the positive parenting strategies in front of your practitioner. You were also able to refine your parenting plans by monitoring your behavior, noticing what you're doing well and what you'd like to do differently, and setting goals for change.

homework

- Make a note of the homework tasks you would like to complete before your next session.

- Skills to practice:

....

....

....

....

- Other homework tasks and suggested reading:

....

....

....

....

- It is a good idea to continue to keep track of your child's behavior and plot this data on your behavior graph. Stop monitoring once the behavior has reached a level you are happy with for 5 days. You can then start keeping track of another behavior if you like.
- Before your next practice session, set goals for the practice task and note them down in Exercise 1 on page 98.

what's next?

The next session will give you another chance to track your use of the positive parenting strategies. You will be prompted to set some specific goals for the practice task, and think about what you are doing well and what you could improve on, and set further goals for change.

For the next appointment, both parents (where applicable) should be available with your child.

The next appointment is at home/the clinic at (time) ....

on (day and date) ....

using positive parenting strategies 3

introduction

This practice session may be held in your home or in the clinic. It is usually the final practice session. The goals for this session will often be related to the skills you have been practicing over the past few days. Remember to set your goals before your practitioner arrives. Aim to build on what happened in the last session. Again, you will be prompted to track how you go, think about what you are doing well and what you could improve on, and set further goals for change.

By the end of Session 7, you should be able to:

- Use positive parenting strategies with your child.
- Monitor your use of positive parenting strategies.
- Notice what you are doing well in using positive parenting strategies and what you could improve on.
- Set specific goals for further practice.

getting started

To help the practice session run as smoothly as possible, please follow these guidelines if the session is in your home:

- Turn the television, DVD and computer games off during the practice session.
- Keep incoming telephone calls brief and do not make any outgoing calls.
- Keep all family members in the same area during the practice task so your practitioner can easily see and hear what is happening.
- Do not speak to your practitioner during the practice task.

practice task

■ exercise 1 setting goals for the practice task

List your goals for today's practice task — be as specific as you can.

....

....

....

....

■ exercise 2 keeping track of what you do

During the practice task, you may like to use the checklists on the following pages to remind yourself of the steps for dealing with some common problem behaviors or a target behavior you have discussed with your practitioner. You can also refer to them after the practice task to see how well you went. These checklists can help you work out which steps you follow well and any steps you may have forgotten or need to practice. This can help when you are setting goals for change. You can also use the checklists at other times if any of these problems happen. Extra copies of these checklists are included in the Worksheets section.

checklist for managing interrupting

Instructions: When your child has interrupted a conversation or activity, write Yes, No or NA (Not Applicable) for each of the steps below.

STEPS TO FOLLOW	DAY					
	STEPS COMPLETED?					
1. Get your child's attention.						
2. Tell your child what to stop doing and what to do instead — *Stop interrupting. Say "Excuse me" and wait until I am free.*						
3. If your child does as you ask, when there is a break in your activity, praise them for waiting and give them your attention.						
4. If your child does not do as you have asked, tell them what they have done wrong — *You are still interrupting* — and the consequence — *Now go to quiet time.* If necessary, take them to quiet time. Don't argue about it.						
5. If your child does not sit quietly in quiet time, tell them what they have done wrong — *You are not being quiet in quiet time* — and the consequence — *Now you must go to time-out.* Take them straight to time-out.						
6. When your child has been quiet for the set time in quiet time or time-out, help them find something to do.						
7. As soon as possible, praise your child for behaving well.						
NUMBER OF STEPS COMPLETED:						

checklist for managing fighting or not sharing

Instructions: When fighting or not sharing or taking turns with other children happens, record Yes, No or NA (Not Applicable) for each of the steps below.

STEPS TO FOLLOW	DAY STEPS COMPLETED?						
1. Get your child's attention.							
2. Tell your child what to stop doing and what to do instead — *Stop fighting over the game. Take turns please.*							
3. Praise the children if they do as you ask.							
4. If the problem continues, tell your child what they have done wrong and the logical consequence — *You are not taking turns, I'm putting the game away for 5 minutes.* Don't argue about it.							
5. If your child complains, use planned ignoring.							
6. When the time is up, return the activity.							
7. As soon as possible, praise the children for sharing and taking turns.							
8. If the problem happens again, repeat the logical consequence for a longer time or use quiet time.							
NUMBER OF STEPS COMPLETED:							

session 7

checklist for managing aggression

Instructions: When aggression happens, record Yes, No or NA (Not Applicable) for each of the steps below.

STEPS TO FOLLOW	DAY						
	STEPS COMPLETED?						
1. Get your child's attention.							
2. Tell your child what to stop doing and what to do instead — *Stop hitting. Keep your hands to yourself.*							
3. Praise your child if they do as you ask.							
4. If your child does not do as you have asked, tell them what they have done wrong — *You are still hitting* — and the consequence — *Now go to quiet time.* If necessary, take them to quiet time. Don't argue about it.							
5. If your child does not sit quietly in quiet time, tell them what they have done wrong — *You are not being quiet in quiet time* — and the consequence — *Now you must go to time-out.* Take them straight to time-out.							
6. When your child has been quiet for the set time in quiet time or time-out, help them find something to do.							
7. As soon as possible, praise your child for behaving well.							
NUMBER OF STEPS COMPLETED:							

session 7

checklist for managing temper outbursts

Instructions: When temper outbursts (e.g. screaming, crying or stamping feet) happen, record Yes, No or NA (Not Applicable) for each of the steps below.

STEPS TO FOLLOW	DAY							
	STEPS COMPLETED?							
EITHER A) Use planned ignoring for toddlers under 2 years old. OR B) Get your child's attention as best you can and follow the steps below:								
1. Tell your child what to stop doing and what to do instead — *Stop screaming right now. Use a nice voice.*								
2. Praise your child if they do as you ask.								
3. If your child does not do as you have asked, tell them what they have done wrong — *You have not done as I asked* — and the consequence — *Now go to time-out.* Don't argue about it. Take them straight to time-out.								
4. When your child has been quiet for the set time in time-out, help them find something to do.								
5. As soon as possible, praise your child for behaving well.								
NUMBER OF STEPS COMPLETED:								

session 7

checklist for managing whining

Instructions: When whining for something happens, record Yes, No or NA (Not Applicable) for each of the steps below.

STEPS TO FOLLOW	DAY						
	STEPS COMPLETED?						
1. Get your child's attention.							
2. Tell your child what to stop doing and what to do instead — *Stop whining for a piece of cake. Please ask nicely.*							
3. Praise your child if they do as you ask.							
4. If your child does not do as you have asked, tell them what they have done wrong — *You have not asked nicely* — and the consequence — *The cake goes away for 10 minutes.* Try again then. Don't argue about it.							
5. If your child complains, use planned ignoring.							
6. When the time is up, if your child has stopped whining, praise them for being quiet and give them a chance to ask nicely for what they want.							
7. If your child asks nicely, praise them for asking nicely and respond to their request.							
8. If the problem happens again, repeat the logical consequence for a longer time or use quiet time.							
NUMBER OF STEPS COMPLETED:							

session 7

checklist for managing problem behavior

Instructions: When problem behavior happens, record Yes, No or NA (Not Applicable) for each of the steps below.

STEPS TO FOLLOW	DAY							
	STEPS COMPLETED?							
NUMBER OF STEPS COMPLETED:								

session 7

■ exercise 3 reviewing the practice task

What do you feel *you* did well during the practice task? Refer to the goals you set in Exercise 1. Which goals did you achieve?

....

....

....

....

....

....

....

What do you feel *you* could have done differently to improve on this practice task? Think about the goals you set in Exercise 1. Was there a goal you did not reach?

....

....

....

....

....

....

....

....

session 7

other issues

You may like to use the space below to make notes about any other issues discussed in the session.

....

....

....

....

....

....

conclusion

In today's session, you had another chance to use the positive parenting strategies in front of your practitioner. You were also able to refine your parenting plans by monitoring your behavior, noticing what you're doing well and what you'd like to do differently, and setting goals for change.

homework

- Make a note of the homework tasks you would like to complete before your next session.

- Skills to practice:

....

....

....

- Other homework tasks and suggested reading:

....

....

....

- It is a good idea to continue to keep track of your child's behavior and plot this data on your behavior graph. Stop monitoring once the behavior has reached a level you are happy with for 5 days. You can then start keeping track of another behavior if you like.

- In preparation for the next session, read through Session 8 in your workbook. As you work through this material, try to note down some ideas for each of the exercises. You will be able to discuss these ideas at your next appointment.

- If available, watch the Going Shopping section of the *Every Parent's Guide to Preschoolers* DVD.

what's next?

In Session 8 you will be introduced to a strategy called planned activities for dealing with 'high-risk' situations in which children's behavior can be particularly difficult to manage.

For the next appointment, both parents (where applicable) should attend without your child if possible. If you are unable to arrange alternative child care for your child, bring some toys and activities to keep your child busy during the session.

The next appointment is at home/the clinic at (time) ....

on (day and date) ....

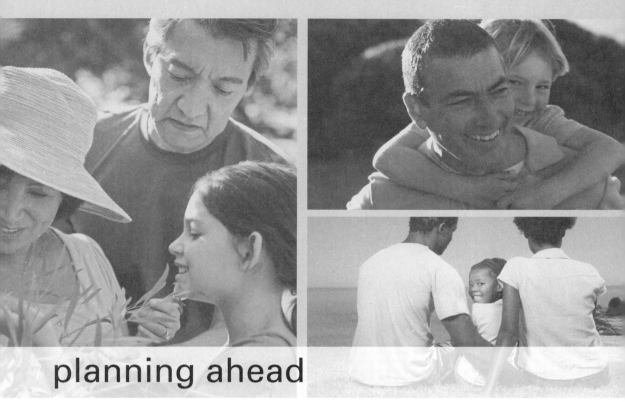

planning ahead

introduction

At this point, you may find that your child's behavior is improving. However, there are often 'high-risk' times or places when managing your child's behavior can be more difficult. These situations are often not designed for children, like when few activities or toys are available and children don't have anything to do. Other high-risk times are when parents have to do too many things at once, or when they have time pressure, like getting ready for school and work on time. Some common high-risk situations include going shopping, visiting friends or relatives, waiting in line (e.g. at the bank), and getting ready to go out. In these situations, a little planning ahead can help. In this session you will look at how to apply planned activities routines to your own high-risk situations. You will also have a chance to review changes in your child's and your own behavior since starting Standard Triple P.

By the end of Session 8, you should be able to:

* Note high-risk situations at home and in the community when your child is more likely to be difficult to manage.
* Design, use and monitor your own planned activities routines for two high-risk situations.

update on progress

▧ exercise 1 reviewing progress

List any improvements in your child's and your own behavior that have happened since starting Standard Triple P. You may find it helpful to refer to the goals for change you set in Session 2, on page 32 of this workbook.

CHANGES IN YOUR CHILD'S BEHAVIOR	CHANGES IN YOUR OWN BEHAVIOR

List any things in your child's and your own behavior that are worse since starting Standard Triple P.

CHANGES IN YOUR CHILD'S BEHAVIOR	CHANGES IN YOUR OWN BEHAVIOR

List any child problem behaviors that do not seem to have changed since starting Standard Triple P.

....

....

....

high-risk situations

▨ exercise 2 identifying high-risk parenting situations

Think of times that are high risk for you. Place a check next to those home and community situations listed below that can be high-risk times for your family. There is space at the bottom for you to add in other high-risk situations. Rate how confident you are that you can deal with your child's behavior in each situation (from 1 *not at all confident* to 10 *extremely confident*).

Home situations	✔	Rating
• waking, getting out of bed	☐	☐
• getting dressed	☐	☐
• eating breakfast, lunch or dinner	☐	☐
• using the bathroom or toilet	☐	☐
• when you are busy (e.g. cooking, talking to someone)	☐	☐
• getting ready to go out (e.g. to school)	☐	☐
• when visitors arrive	☐	☐
• playing indoors or outdoors	☐	☐
• watching television	☐	☐
• when you are on the telephone	☐	☐
• while you are preparing meals	☐	☐
• after school	☐	☐
• when a parent comes home from work	☐	☐
• undressing/getting ready for bed	☐	☐
• bedtime	☐	☐
•	☐	☐
•	☐	☐
•	☐	☐

Community situations	✔	Rating
• visiting friends or relatives	☐	☐
• going on family outings (e.g. beach)	☐	☐
• parties	☐	☐
• weddings/funerals	☐	☐
• holidays	☐	☐
• going out for dinner	☐	☐

	✔	Rating
• going to the doctor/dentist	☐	☐
• traveling in the car	☐	☐
• traveling on public transport	☐	☐
• shopping at the supermarket	☐	☐
• going to a shopping center	☐	☐
• going to the bank	☐	☐
• leaving your child at a daycare/school	☐	☐
• leaving your child with other caregivers	☐	☐
•	☐	☐
•	☐	☐
•	☐	☐

planned activities

By planning and problem solving ahead of time for your high-risk situations you can avoid problems. The main ideas are to plan some interesting activities for your child so they are less likely to get bored and misbehave, and to be clear about what you would like your child to do.

At first you may like to have some practice. Choose a time to try out the new routine in your high-risk situation and show your child how it works. Make sure you are not busy with other things. Think about when you could have a practice run, where it should be and who should be there. Set easy goals at first and work up to more difficult situations (e.g. start by visiting a friend for 10 minutes then build up to longer visits).

The following steps will help you plan for dealing with high-risk situations.

prepare in advance

Think about any advance planning or preparation you could do before the high-risk situation. Have everything ready that you will need (like having some activities ready, drawing up a behavior chart, having stickers and rewards ready, packing bags and preparing food the night before to avoid last minute rushing).

For outings, plan your trip to avoid disrupting your child's routine, such as usual mealtimes and sleep times.

talk about rules

Prepare your child by telling them what is going to happen. Decide on rules for how you expect your child to behave in the situation and calmly talk about the rules with your child (e.g. some rules for traveling on the bus might be: *Stay in your seat, Use a quiet voice, Keep your hands and feet to yourself*). Ask your child to repeat the rules, praise them if they remember and prompt them if they need help. Remind your child of the rules as you enter the high-risk situation.

choose interesting activities

Keep your child busy in the high-risk situation. Make a list of interesting activities. Ask your child to choose some activities of their own. You may need to help them get started. Try to make use of any chances to have fun together and use incidental teaching to keep your child interested and playing longer (e.g. talk to your child, ask them questions, count or name things you see, play games like 'I spy').

use rewards for good behavior

List rewards for following the rules. Make sure the rewards are practical and you can give them right away. You may find it useful to prepare a special behavior chart for some high-risk situations. Explain the rewards to your child when you explain the rules. Ask if your child has any other ideas for rewards or any questions, and praise them for helping with this advance planning. Praise your child often for good behavior in the high-risk situation and give the reward if the rules are followed (e.g. going to the park on the way home).

use consequences for misbehavior

Decide on some consequences for failing to follow the rules. Explain these consequences to your child when you explain the rules and rewards. Make sure the consequences are practical and immediate (e.g. quiet time at the store may involve having your child sit quietly where they are, and if the problem behavior gets worse, you may need to have your child sit outside the store or in the car while you wait beside them).

have a follow-up discussion

Afterwards, talk with your child about how things went. Praise your child for following the rules, and if necessary, describe one rule your child forgot to follow. Discuss anything either you or your child think still needs to be changed, and set a goal for next time (e.g. *You did really well staying close to me while we were at the bank today, but next time let's see if you can remember to use a quiet voice in the bank*).

A sample routine for grocery shopping at the supermarket is presented on page 115. This routine shows how all the steps fit together to make a planned activities routine.

example planned activities routine

Note the high-risk situation

- Grocery shopping at the supermarket

Note details for a practice session (when, where, who should be there)

- A short trip to get bread, milk and fruit at the local supermarket
- Mom and one child to be present

List any planning or preparation

- Avoid disrupting sleep and mealtimes
- Pack a small snack and drink
- Prepare a shopping list

Decide on rules

- Stay close
- Only touch things when Mom says to
- Walk quietly

Choose interesting activities

- Having their own shopping list
- Finding products
- Putting things in the basket
- Talking about colors, prices, shapes, sizes
- Holding the shopping list, keys or wallets

List rewards for good behavior

- Praise
- Carrying the basket
- Special activity with a parent (e.g. trip to the park)

List consequences for misbehavior

- Clear, calm instruction to stop the problem behavior and what to do instead
- Quiet time in the aisle, shopping center or car park
- No reward

Note any goals from the follow-up discussion

- Stay close

▨ exercise 3 developing a planned activities routine

Now you have the chance to design your own planned activities routine on the blank sheet on page 116. Work through one of the high-risk situations you noted on the checklist on pages 112–113.

planned activities routine

Note the high-risk situation

Note details for a practice session (when, where, who should be there)

List any planning or preparation

Decide on rules

Choose interesting activities

List rewards for good behavior

List consequences for misbehavior

Note any goals from the follow-up discussion

conclusion

Following a review of your progress so far, six steps for planning a parenting routine for a high-risk situation were presented:

- preparing in advance
- talking about rules
- choosing interesting activities
- using rewards for good behavior
- using consequences for misbehavior
- having a follow-up discussion

homework

- Choose two of your own high-risk situations and develop planned activities routines for each of them. There are two blank *Planned Activities Routine* forms on pages 119 and 120. Try out two of your routines at least once in the coming week. There are two monitoring forms on pages 121 and 122. To complete these forms, write down each step in your routine and then note whether or not you completed it in the high-risk situation. Extra copies of these forms are in the Worksheets section. Write down the two high-risk situations you plan to try out this week.

....

....

....

....

- It is a good idea to continue to keep track of your child's behavior. Stop monitoring once the behavior has reached a level you are happy with for 5 days or so. You can then start keeping track of another behavior if you like.

- In preparation for Session 9, use your advanced planning skills to prepare a planned activities routine for encouraging independent play when you are busy. You may need to bring a number of things (e.g. stickers, activities) to the session with you so that you can put your plan into action. Write down each of the steps in your routine on the monitoring form on page 121. You can use this checklist to track how you go at encouraging independent play in the next session. Prepare in advance for this task by deciding on rules for your child, bringing interesting activities to the session, as well as rewards and consequences to back up your rules. Talk with your child before the session about what you expect, what will happen if they follow the rules and what will happen if they do not follow the rules.

- In Session 9 you will also be asked to set up a fun activity to do with your child for about 15 minutes. Think about an activity you think your child would enjoy (e.g. toy play, making something together, planning a family activity), and bring along anything you will need (e.g. art materials, painting shirts).
- Plan an outing for right after the next session. In Exercise 6 on page 129, list where you will go and the rules, rewards and consequences you have decided on.

what's next?

In Session 9 you will have a chance to review how successful your planned activities routines have been and to continue to design more routines for high-risk situations. By bringing your child to the next session, you will be able to practice the planned activities routine for encouraging your child to play independently, as well as incidental teaching and discussing rules with your child when getting ready to go out. During the session, you will track your strengths in using these strategies and anything you could improve on. It may be helpful to review the description of incidental teaching on page 42. In preparation for the rule discussion, think about where you could go immediately after your next session and what rules would be appropriate.

For the next appointment, both parents (where applicable) should attend with your child.

The next appointment is at home/the clinic at (time) ....

on (day and date) ....

planned activities routine

Note the high-risk situation

Note details for a practice session (when, where, who should be there)

List any planning or preparation

Decide on rules

Choose interesting activities

List rewards for good behavior

List consequences for misbehavior

Note any goals from the follow-up discussion

planned activities routine

Note the high-risk situation

....

Note details for a practice session (when, where, who should be there)

....

....

List any planning or preparation

....

....

Decide on rules

....

....

....

Choose interesting activities

....

....

....

List rewards for good behavior

....

....

....

List consequences for misbehavior

....

....

....

Note any goals from the follow-up discussion

....

....

....

planned activities checklist

Situation: ....

Instructions: Whenever this situation happens record Yes, No or NA (Not Applicable)
for each of the steps below.

STEPS TO FOLLOW	DAY						
	STEPS COMPLETED?						
1.							
2.							
3.							
4.							
5.							
6.							
NUMBER OF STEPS COMPLETED:							

planned activities checklist

Situation: ....

Instructions: Whenever this situation happens record Yes, No or NA (Not Applicable) for each of the steps below.

	DAY						
STEPS TO FOLLOW	**STEPS COMPLETED?**						
1.							
2.							
3.							
4.							
5.							
6.							
NUMBER OF STEPS COMPLETED:							

session 8

using planned activities routines

introduction

During this session you will have a chance to practice three planned activities routines. To start, you will prepare your child to play independently or get involved in a quiet activity while you are busy with your practitioner. Then, using the fun activity you brought with you to this session, you will be able to have some quality time with your child. To finish, you will be prompted to use the planned activities routine for getting ready to go out. As part of these practice tasks, you will use each of the six steps of the planned activities routine including planning ahead, discussing rules with your child, having interesting activities, backing up rules with rewards and consequences, and holding a follow-up discussion. To help the session run smoothly, use your planning skills to prepare yourself and your child ahead of time. During the session you will also be able to develop a planned activities routine for another high-risk situation.

By the end of Session 9, you should be able to:

- Use planned activities routines in a variety of situations including when you are busy and when you are going out.
- Design, use and monitor planned activities routines for high-risk situations as required.

- Use positive parenting strategies such as incidental teaching, attention and praise to encourage your child's independent play.
- Use positive parenting strategies to deal with interrupting.
- Find information on parenting issues, if needed.

encouraging independent play

■ exercise 1 preparing your child for independent play

For the first part of this session, you will talk with your practitioner while your child plays independently or is involved in an interesting activity. This situation is similar to when you visit other adults who do not have children. In this exercise you will have a chance to follow all six steps of your planned activities routine for encouraging independent play while you are busy. You may find it helpful to refer to your *Planned Activities Checklist* on page 125.

At the start of the session, prepare your child by reminding them of what to expect in this situation as well as the rules, rewards and consequences that you have decided on. Then take a few minutes to get your child started on an activity before returning your attention to your practitioner. Remember to interrupt your practitioner every now and again to praise your child and take an interest in their activity. If necessary, your practitioner will prompt you to attend to your child at regular intervals. Be prepared to use positive parenting strategies to deal with interruptions from your child.

At the end of this exercise, your practitioner will ask you to think about how well you followed this routine. Think about a couple of things you have done well and things you could have done differently. If necessary, set some goals for next time.

planned activities checklist

Situation: ....

Instructions: Whenever this situation happens record Yes, No or NA (Not Applicable)
for each of the steps below.

STEPS TO FOLLOW	DAY					
	STEPS COMPLETED?					
1.						
2.						
3.						
4.						
5.						
6.						
NUMBER OF STEPS COMPLETED:						

review of homework

■ exercise 2 reviewing your use of planned activities routines

What were your practice tasks from Session 8?

....

....

....

....

What worked? It may be helpful to look at your *Planned Activities Checklist/s*.

....

....

....

....

Is there anything you could have done differently? You may notice some steps on your *Planned Activities Checklist/s* that you missed or could improve.

....

....

....

....

Set yourself some goals for the next time you use these planned activities routines.

....

....

....

....

further planning

■ exercise 3 developing more planned activities routines

During the session, design a planned activities routine for another one of your high-risk situations. A blank form is provided on page 127.

planned activities routine

Note the high-risk situation

....

Note details for a practice session (when, where, who should be there)

....

....

List any planning or preparation

....

....

Decide on rules

....

....

....

Choose interesting activities

....

....

....

List rewards for good behavior

....

....

....

List consequences for misbehavior

....

....

....

Note any goals from the follow-up discussion

....

....

....

■ exercise 4 holding a follow-up discussion

The final step of a planned activities routine involves holding a follow-up discussion with your child about their behavior in the high-risk situation. The aim is to tell your child what they did well in the situation (i.e. what rules your child followed) and, if necessary, to set a goal for what your child could do differently next time (i.e. remind your child about a rule that was not followed).

Talk with your child about how well they went at playing independently while you were busy with your practitioner. Talk to your child about the things they did well and, if necessary, set a goal for next time. Prepare your child for the transition to the next activity. You may need to get your child to clean up some things before moving on to Exercise 5.

engaging activity

■ exercise 5 doing activities together

In this exercise, you will again follow all six steps of a planned activities routine with your child. However, this time you will have more opportunity to practice using positive parenting skills to encourage their involvement in an activity.

Prepare your child by telling them what is going to happen and how long it will take. Talk to your child about the rules for your chosen activity as well as rewards and consequences to back up your rules. Do whatever is needed to set up the room for your activity (e.g. move the furniture, put newspaper down if using paints). During the activity, use positive parenting strategies such as talking with your child, praise and incidental teaching to encourage your child's involvement with the activity. After 10 to 15 minutes, prepare your child for the transition to the next activity. You will need to get your child to help clean up this activity before moving on to Exercise 6.

At the end of this exercise, your practitioner will ask you to think about how well you followed this routine. Think about a couple of things you did well and things you could do differently. If necessary, set some goals for next time.

getting ready to go out

Preparing children in advance for new situations is the first step in any planned activities routine. Problems can often be avoided when children know what is going to happen and what is expected of them. The next exercise gives you a chance to practice preparing your child and discussing rules with your child as you get ready for an outing. In preparation for this exercise, think about where you can go after your session. Then think about the rules you would like to discuss with your child as well as rewards and consequences you can use to back up your rules.

▧ exercise 6 discussing rules with your child

Where do you plan to go after this session?

List the rules you will discuss with your child.

What rewards can your child earn for following the rules?

What consequences will you use if your child does not follow the rules?

After discussing the rules with your child, your practitioner will prompt you to think about how you went: what you did well and anything you would do differently. If necessary, set some goals for next time.

session 9

conclusion

Today's session gave you a chance to use planned activities routines in different situations. You used positive parenting strategies such as incidental teaching, praise and attending to your child to encourage their involvement in activities. You also tracked how you went in using these positive parenting skills and whether there is anything you'd like to improve on.

homework

- Use two of your planned activities routines before your next session. There are two monitoring forms on pages 131 and 132. To complete these forms, write down each step of your routine and then note whether or not you completed it in the high-risk situation. Extra copies of these forms are included in the Worksheets section. Write down the two high-risk situations you plan to practice this week.

....

....

....

....

- Keep track of the same behavior you began monitoring after Session 1. This will help you see what changes have happened in your child's behavior since beginning Standard Triple P.
- In preparation for the next session, read through Session 10 in your workbook. and, if available, watch *Every Parent's Survival Guide*:
  • Part 5, Family Survival Tips
- As you work through this material, try to note down a few ideas for each of the exercises. You will be able to discuss these ideas at your next appointment.

what's next?

The final session will look at what has changed since you started Standard Triple P and whether you have reached the goals you set at the beginning of the program. The session will also give some ideas on how to keep things going after the Triple P sessions have finished.

For the next appointment, both parents (where applicable) should attend without your child if possible. If you are unable to arrange alternative child care for your child, bring some toys and activities to keep your child busy during the session.

The next appointment is at home/the clinic at (time) ....

on (day and date) ....

planned activities checklist

Situation: ....

Instructions: Whenever this situation happens record Yes, No or NA (Not Applicable) for each of the steps below.

			DAY				
STEPS TO FOLLOW			**STEPS COMPLETED?**				
1.							
2.							
3.							
4.							
5.							
6.							
NUMBER OF STEPS COMPLETED:							

planned activities checklist

Situation: ....

Instructions: Whenever this situation happens record Yes, No or NA (Not Applicable) for each of the steps below.

STEPS TO FOLLOW	DAY						
	STEPS COMPLETED?						
1.							
2.							
3.							
4.							
5.							
6.							
NUMBER OF STEPS COMPLETED:							

session 9

program close

introduction

This session looks at family survival tips and ways to keep up the good changes you have made during the program. Keeping up these improvements over the long term is important. You will also review your family's progress through Standard Triple P, and come up with some parenting routines for more high-risk situations. At the end of this session, you will complete a booklet of questionnaires like the one you did at the start of the program. These forms help show what changes have happened in both your own and your child's behavior as a result of completing Standard Triple P.

By the end of Session 10, you should be able to:

- Use family survival tips to help make the task of parenting easier.
- Use a range of positive parenting strategies at home and in the community.
- Develop parenting plans for high-risk situations.
- Identify changes in your child's and your own behavior since starting Standard Triple P.
- Keep up the changes made so far.
- Set further goals for change in both your child's and your own behavior and decide how to achieve these goals.

review of homework

■ exercise 1 reviewing your use of planned activities routines

What were your practice tasks from Session 9?

....

....

....

....

What worked? It may be helpful to look at your *Planned Activities Checklist/s.*

....

....

....

....

Is there anything you could have done differently? You may notice some steps on your *Planned Activities Checklist/s* that you missed or could improve.

....

....

....

....

Set yourself some goals for the next time you use these planned activities routines.

....

....

....

....

family survival tips

It is easier to look after your child's needs if you also look after your own. Here are some more ideas that can help make parenting easier.

work as a team

Parenting is easier when parents and other carers support each other and agree on how to manage misbehavior. Support and back up each other's parenting efforts. Before you use new strategies, discuss the plan with your partner and anyone else in a caring role with your child. Talk to each other about any disagreements you have about handling your child's behavior. Help each other out when you can.

avoid arguments in front of your child

Children know when there is conflict between people around them. It can upset them if they see a lot of arguing and fighting and disagreements are not settled. If there is something you strongly disagree about, try to talk about it when your child is not there.

get support

Everyone needs help and support in rearing children. Partners, family, friends and neighbors can all be good supports. Talk about your ideas and compare experiences. You may like to continue to meet with other parents from your group. It is also a good idea to have someone from the group to contact regularly for support and to talk about how things are going.

have a break

All parents need some time away from their children. This is normal and healthy. If you give plenty of positive attention and have quality time together, it will not harm your child if you have a break now and then and leave them with someone you trust. It is the quality of time you spend together that is important, not the amount of time.

session 10

■ exercise 2 taking care of yourself

Who do you go to for support?

Family ....

Friends ....

What can you do to get more support, if needed?

....

....

....

Make a note of things you like to do for yourself (on your own or with your partner, family or friends).

....

....

....

Think about when you can have a break over the next week and who you can call on to look after your child.

....

....

phasing out the program

During the course of this program, a number of things have been introduced into your life that are unlikely to occur naturally in your family life. Examples include homework tasks, keeping records of your own and your child's behavior, and reading this workbook. Part of finishing a program means giving these up and going back to normal. This does not mean going back to everything that you were doing before the program. The goal now is to give up the artificial procedures from the program, without going back to old habits. Some steps are suggested below to help you do this.

put away the program materials

Put the program materials away somewhere handy so you can pull them out to look at from time to time. You may choose to mark or take out those sections of the program materials that have been the most useful so they are easy to find if you need them.

phase out monitoring

Throughout the program, you have been asked to keep track or monitor what you have been doing and what your child has been doing. In everyday life, most people do not keep ongoing records like this. If you are currently keeping track of your progress, decide how well-established your new routines are. If you feel you can continue your new behavior without keeping a record, it is time to stop recording. If you are less certain, start to phase out the recording. Monitor your own or your child's behavior less often, such as once a week rather than each day, and aim to phase monitoring out completely when you feel confident of your progress.

phase out specific strategies

Look at the types of strategies you have in place, such as behavior charts. Decide whether these can be simplified and phased out over time. Some of the suggestions we have made, such as praising a child very often for a particular behavior, are most useful for changing behavior. To keep the good changes going, it is best to reward behaviors unpredictably once in a while, and not every time the behavior happens.

Gradually make changes to behavior charts and rewards. Make sure there are still plenty of rewarding things in your child's life. Behavior problems can reappear if children do not get enough encouragement and support for good behavior.

review your progress regularly

During this program, you have paid attention to your family's problems and goals on a daily or weekly basis. This can be relaxed a bit now. However, it is important to keep up with how your family is going. To pick up any problems or slip-ups early, have a progress review at least once a month.

progress review

When you began Standard Triple P, you identified changes you would like to see in your child's behavior as well as in your own behavior.

■ exercise 3 identifying changes that have been made

Take a few minutes to complete the table below, noting the changes that both you and your child have made since starting the program. It may help to look back at your goals on page 32 of this workbook.

CHANGES IN YOUR CHILD'S BEHAVIOR	CHANGES IN YOUR OWN BEHAVIOR

Congratulations on the changes you have made yourself and the changes you have helped your child to make.

keeping up the good changes

obstacles to maintaining change

Here are some common reasons for not maintaining improvements made through a program like Triple P.

family transitions

Triple P has helped you to make changes in dealing with your child's behavior. The changes you have made are designed to suit your family as it is now. However, families change over time. They grow and develop, and change in size. Common changes families experience include the birth of a child, a parent changing employment status (like going back to work, taking on extra work, becoming unemployed), changes in family structure (like parents separating or entering new relationships) and children growing older and moving through new stages.

children's stages as they grow up

The types of child behavior problems faced by parents change as children grow older (e.g. from toddler tantrums to shyness at preschool to problems with schoolwork). Successful parenting requires being flexible over time. As different problems arise, the strategies you use for dealing with them will need to change. This is why recommended ages are provided with the positive parenting strategies described in Sessions 3 and 4. Strategies that are useful now with your child may not be as helpful in 6 months or 6 years time. The good news is that, no matter how old your child is, the basic principles remain the same. Children will continue to do well in an environment that provides them with love, support and predictability.

high-risk times

There are likely to be times in your life when it will be difficult to keep up the changes you have made as part of Triple P. Research suggests that the quality of family life tends to decrease during periods of stress. These periods of stress are known as high-risk times. For example, a death in the family, a serious illness, job loss or other major upheaval, all affect how family members feel and get along with one another. These events are likely to affect things like the way parents talk with their children, their time spent with others, their tolerance of misbehavior, and their ability to plan for and deal with problems. These are the times when parents may fail to use positive parenting strategies for dealing with family problems and be likely to revert to old habits and unhelpful approaches. Some common high-risk times include:

- changes in family finances
- times when parents are feeling depressed
- times of family conflict
- moving house
- when parents are stressed at work
- changing schools
- death or illness in the family
- involvement in court action

Another high-risk time for many people is immediately after the end of a program such as Triple P. Unfortunately, just because the program is finished, it does not mean all the hard work is over.

ideas for keeping up the good changes

With planning and care, you can avoid many of the problems that can come up because of family changes, high-risk times and changes associated with children growing older. There are four key steps to overcoming obstacles to keeping up the good changes and avoiding slip-ups.

plan for high-risk times

A good way to avoid problems involves planning to deal with potentially difficult times before any trouble starts. Just as you plan ways to keep your child busy and out of trouble during an outing, you need to plan for future situations where problems may arise. You can start now. Later in the session, you will spend some time thinking of possible high-risk situations that may come up in the next 6 months. Problem solving ways of dealing with these situations before they arise can help minimize problems.

review your family's progress

If you review your family's progress regularly it is more likely that you will be able to notice problems as they arise. You will also be able to take appropriate action to prevent any further problems. Review your progress every 2 weeks at first, then once a month.

act quickly if problems happen

It is important to do something right away if things do start to get worse. You may decide to start specific parenting strategies again (such as planned activities routines or behavior charts). It may be helpful to go back to the program material to check strategies or look for new ideas.

try new ways

If existing strategies are no longer working, try out new things. Look at what you already know — give your child lots of attention and encouragement when they are behaving well and remove your attention when they misbehave. Try to find ways of adapting strategies to new situations. Try out the new way for a week or two, keep track of how successful it is, and continue or refine the routine if necessary. Some guidelines for choosing appropriate consequences are outlined below.

- *Consequences should relate to the misbehavior.* When consequences are directly related to misbehavior, children learn what they have done wrong. For example, when children fight over a toy, removing the toy from both children will help them to learn that fighting over toys is not acceptable. When you can't think of a consequence that directly relates to the misbehavior, consider withdrawing a privilege and explaining why you are doing so.

- *Consequences should provide an incentive for good behavior.* To encourage children to behave well, they need to be given the opportunity to do so. For example, grounding a child for 3 weeks for coming home late gives them no chance or reason to behave well in the near future. A better consequence may be: for each 5 minutes they are late, they lose half an hour off the time they must be home the next day (not late = allowed out till 5.00 pm the next day; 5 minutes late = home by 4.30 pm; 10 minutes late = home by 4.00 pm). These consequences give children an incentive to try to be home on time the next day. For a child who will not turn off the television to do homework, rather than a 2-week ban from watching television, only allow television each night after homework has been completed.

- *Consequences should be appropriate to children's age and developmental stage.* Change consequences to suit the age and abilities of your child. For example, with younger children consequences are generally shorter than for older children. Older children will respond to consequences such as cutting down an allowance, extra chores, less computer time, less play time and less time spent with friends after school.

- *Consequences should not threaten a child's sense of worth or self-esteem.* Consequences that are harsh, too long, or involve physical or verbal punishment can be damaging to your child. Many children who misbehave also have low self-esteem, or are anxious or depressed. Punishments can make these children feel worse about themselves. Avoid consequences that single your child out (for example, take your child out of the room rather than dealing with a problem in front of others), stop siblings teasing a child in time-out, and avoid shaming or criticizing your child.

- *Consequences should be enforceable.* Do not threaten a consequence unless you are prepared to carry it out. For example, if you tell your child they can't come on a family day trip because they have misbehaved, then you must be prepared to follow through with this action and arrange for someone to take care of your child while the rest of the family goes out.

- *Consequences should be carried out immediately.* Children learn more quickly, and can connect their actions to the consequences, if consequences happen right away. For example, if your child is disruptive during a long car trip, stop the car and put them into quiet time rather than waiting until you get to where you are going before you use a consequence.

- *Consequences should be used consistently.* Children are more likely to learn the results of their actions if they receive the same consequences each time a problem occurs. It is also helpful if different adults do the same thing. To prevent children from feeling picked on, make sure all children are treated alike. Provide similar consequences for all children in your family, although you may need to make changes to suit the age of your child. Use consequences consistently and ignore excuses from children. This will discourage them from complaining and arguing with your decisions.

problem solving for the future

■ exercise 4 planning for future high-risk times

Spend a few minutes planning possible solutions to these situations. Discuss your ideas with your practitioner and make notes if you like. What would you do if...

Your 8-year-old has been in trouble the last 3 weekends at football for yelling at his team mates. You are worried he will be removed from the team if his temper outbursts continue.

Your 11-year-old is being bullied at school. Two children have started to call her names and exclude her from their games. She is coming home after school in tears and complains of feeling sick before school each day. She is also starting to call herself names (such as Stupid and Ugly) and saying she's not good at doing anything.

The school holidays start in 3 weeks time. You will have your three school-age children home with you each day for weeks and you expect arguments and complaints of being bored.

▮ exercise 5 identifying future high-risk times

Discuss with your practitioner any high-risk times that may come up in the next 6 months (like going to the dentist, starting a new school, a parent starting part-time work). List them below.

▮ exercise 6 independent problem solving

Using the blank form on page 144, design a routine for dealing with one of the potential high-risk times you have just thought of.

planned activities checklist

Situation: ....

Instructions: Whenever this situation happens record Yes, No or NA (Not Applicable)
for each of the steps below.

STEPS TO FOLLOW	DAY						
	STEPS COMPLETED?						
1.							
2.							
3.							
4.							
5.							
6.							
NUMBER OF STEPS COMPLETED:							

future goals

■ exercise 7 setting future goals

Spend a few minutes thinking about any further goals you have about your parenting skills and your child's behavior. Discuss your goals with your practitioner and record them in the space below. How could you work towards these new goals?

....

....

....

....

....

....

final assessment

■ exercise 8 completing *Assessment Booklet Two*

Now that you have completed the program, your practitioner will give you a copy of *Assessment Booklet Two* to complete. These are the same forms you completed at the start of the program. The aim is to find out what has changed during the program and whether the program has met your family's needs. Please take some time to complete the questionnaires, thinking about how things are at the moment.

conclusion

Today's session introduced family survival tips to help make the task of parenting easier. You reviewed the positive changes that have happened since you started Triple P and discussed how to keep up those changes. You planned some ways to prevent problems in future high-risk situations. You also thought about goals for the future and how you can achieve your goals.

homework

• Put your Standard Triple P materials away somewhere handy and start to phase out any monitoring records or checklists you are using.
• Continue to use your positive parenting strategies and your parenting routines for high-risk situations.
• Make a note of any other homework tasks or reading you would like to complete.

....

....

....

....

congratulations

You have now completed Standard Triple P. Congratulations on staying interested and involved throughout the program. We hope you have enjoyed the program and are enjoying the benefits of positive parenting. Keep up the good work. As your child continues to grow, different situations and new problems are bound to arise. Refer back to your workbook and other Triple P resources at any time to review the strategies you have learned or to look up ideas for dealing with a new problem behavior. If you have any concerns in the future about your child's progress or any family issues, seek professional advice. Thank you for participating in Triple P. We hope you found it enjoyable and worthwhile.

worksheets

You can make copies of these worksheets to use with your workbook. Remember to keep the originals so you can make extra copies if you want them.

behavior diary

Instructions: List the problem behavior, when and where it happened, and what happened before and after.

Problem behavior: .... Day: ....

PROBLEM	WHEN AND WHERE DID IT HAPPEN?	WHAT HAPPENED BEFORE?	WHAT HAPPENED AFTER?	OTHER COMMENTS

worksheets

tally

Instructions: Write the day in the first column, then place a mark in the next column each time the behavior happens on that day. Record the total number for each day in the end column.

Behavior: _____   Starting date: _____

DAY	1	2	3	4	5	6	7	8	9	10	11	12	13	14	15	TOTAL

product tally

Instructions: Write each behavior outcome at the top of a column. Keep track by writing the day in the first column, then place a mark in the relevant column for each behavior outcome you count on that day.

DAY	BEHAVIOR OUTCOMES			

worksheets

duration record

Instructions: Write the day in the first column, then each time the behavior happens, record how long it lasts in seconds, minutes or hours. Record the total amount of time for each day in the end column.

Behavior: ....

Starting date: ....

DAY	1	2	3	4	5	6	7	8	9	10	TOTAL

worksheets

time sample

Instructions: Choose the time blocks you want to record and write them in the first column. Place a mark in the relevant square if the behavior happens at least once in that time block. Put a dash if the behavior does not happen. Record the total number of marks for each day at the bottom of the column.

Behavior: .... Starting date: ....

TIME	M	T	W	T	F	S	S	M	T	W	T	F	S	S
TOTAL														

momentary time sample

Instructions: Choose the times you want to record and write them in the first column. Place a mark in the relevant square if the behavior is happening at that moment. Put a dash if the behavior is not happening. Record the total number of marks for each day at the bottom of the column.

Behavior: .... Starting date: ....

TIME	M	T	W	T	F	S	S	M	T	W	T	F	S	S
TOTAL														

behavior graph

Instructions: Plot the number of times the behavior happens each day by placing a cross on the appropriate column, then
join up the marks for each day.

Behavior: ....   Month: ....

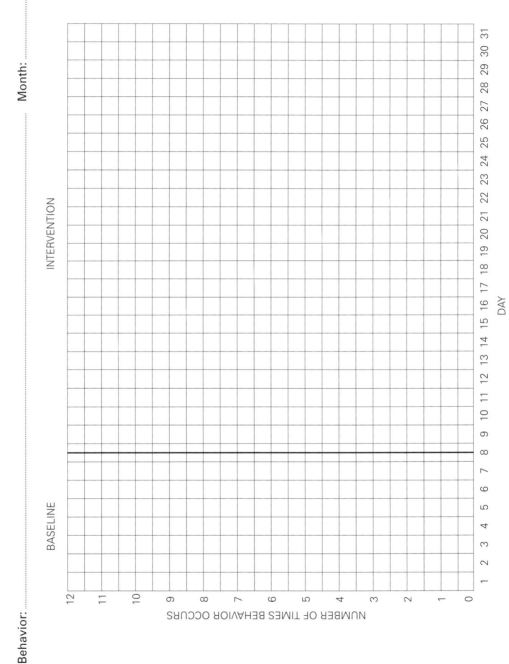

strategies for helping children develop

Choose two of the strategies that you would like to practice with your child over the next week. Be as specific as possible (e.g. one goal may be to use descriptive praise with your child at least five times per day). Use the table below to record whether you reached your goals each day. Note what went well and list any problems that you had.

GOAL 1:

....

....

GOAL 2:

....

....

DAY	GOAL 1 Y/N	GOAL 2 Y/N	COMMENTS
1			
2			
3			
4			
5			
6			
7			

diary of time-out

Instructions: Make a note of the day, the problem behavior, when and where it occurred, and the total length of time your child was in time-out.

Set time for time-out: 2 minutes ☐   3 minutes ☐   4 minutes ☐   5 minutes ☐

DAY	PROBLEM	WHEN AND WHERE IT HAPPENED	LENGTH OF TIME-OUT

checklist for managing interrupting

Instructions: When your child has interrupted a conversation or activity, write Yes, No or NA (Not Applicable) for each of the steps below.

		DAY					
STEPS TO FOLLOW		STEPS COMPLETED?					
1. Get your child's attention.							
2. Tell your child what to stop doing and what to do instead — *Stop interrupting. Say "Excuse me" and wait until I am free.*							
3. If your child does as you ask, when there is a break in your activity, praise them for waiting and give them your attention.							
4. If your child does not do as you have asked, tell them what they have done wrong — *You are still interrupting* — and the consequence — *Now go to quiet time.* If necessary, take them to quiet time. Don't argue about it.							
5. If your child does not sit quietly in quiet time, tell them what they have done wrong — *You are not being quiet in quiet time* — and the consequence — *Now you must go to time-out.* Take them straight to time-out.							
6. When your child has been quiet for the set time in quiet time or time-out, help them find something to do.							
7. As soon as possible, praise your child for behaving well.							
NUMBER OF STEPS COMPLETED:							

worksheets

checklist for managing fighting or not sharing

Instructions: When fighting or not sharing or taking turns with other children happens, record Yes, No or NA (Not Applicable) for each of the steps below.

STEPS TO FOLLOW	DAY						
STEPS COMPLETED?							
1. Get your child's attention.							
2. Tell your child what to stop doing and what to do instead — *Stop fighting over the game. Take turns please.*							
3. Praise the children if they do as you ask.							
4. If the problem continues, tell your child what they have done wrong and the logical consequence — *You are not taking turns, I'm putting the game away for 5 minutes.* Don't argue about it.							
5. If your child complains, use planned ignoring.							
6. When the time is up, return the activity.							
7. As soon as possible, praise the children for sharing and taking turns.							
8. If the problem happens again, repeat the logical consequence for a longer time or use quiet time.							
NUMBER OF STEPS COMPLETED:							

worksheets

checklist for managing aggression

Instructions: When aggression happens, record Yes, No or NA (Not Applicable) for each of the steps below.

STEPS TO FOLLOW	DAY						
	STEPS COMPLETED?						
1. Get your child's attention.							
2. Tell your child what to stop doing and what to do instead — *Stop hitting. Keep your hands to yourself.*							
3. Praise your child if they do as you ask.							
4. If your child does not do as you have asked, tell them what they have done wrong — *You are still hitting* — and the consequence — *Now go to quiet time.* If necessary, take them to quiet time. Don't argue about it.							
5. If your child does not sit quietly in quiet time, tell them what they have done wrong — *You are not being quiet in quiet time* — and the consequence — *Now you must go to time-out.* Take them straight to time-out.							
6. When your child has been quiet for the set time in quiet time or time-out, help them find something to do.							
7. As soon as possible, praise your child for behaving well.							
NUMBER OF STEPS COMPLETED:							

worksheets

checklist for managing temper outbursts

Instructions: When temper outbursts (e.g. screaming, crying or stamping feet) happen, record Yes, No or NA (Not Applicable) for each of the steps below.

STEPS TO FOLLOW	DAY					
	STEPS COMPLETED?					
EITHER A) Use planned ignoring for toddlers under 2 years old. OR B) Get your child's attention as best you can and follow the steps below:						
1. Tell your child what to stop doing and what to do instead — *Stop screaming right now. Use a nice voice.*						
2. Praise your child if they do as you ask.						
3. If your child does not do as you have asked, tell them what they have done wrong — *You have not done as I asked* — and the consequence — *Now go to time-out.* Don't argue about it. Take them straight to time-out.						
4. When your child has been quiet for the set time in time-out, help them find something to do.						
5. As soon as possible, praise your child for behaving well.						
NUMBER OF STEPS COMPLETED:						

worksheets

checklist for managing whining

Instructions: When whining for something happens, record Yes, No or NA (Not Applicable) for each of the steps below.

STEPS TO FOLLOW	DAY — STEPS COMPLETED?						
1. Get your child's attention.							
2. Tell your child what to stop doing and what to do instead — *Stop whining for a piece of cake. Please ask nicely.*							
3. Praise your child if they do as you ask.							
4. If your child does not do as you have asked, tell them what they have done wrong — *You have not asked nicely* — and the consequence — *The cake goes away for 10 minutes.* Try again then. Don't argue about it.							
5. If your child complains, use planned ignoring.							
6. When the time is up, if your child has stopped whining, praise them for being quiet and give them a chance to ask nicely for what they want.							
7. If your child asks nicely, praise them for asking nicely and respond to their request.							
8. If the problem happens again, repeat the logical consequence for a longer time or use quiet time.							
NUMBER OF STEPS COMPLETED:							

checklist for managing problem behavior

Instructions: When problem behavior happens, record Yes, No or NA (Not Applicable) for each of the steps below.

STEPS TO FOLLOW	DAY						
	STEPS COMPLETED?						
NUMBER OF STEPS COMPLETED:							

worksheets

planned activities routine

Note the high-risk situation

_____

Note details for a practice session (when, where, who should be there)

_____

_____

List any planning or preparation

_____

_____

Decide on rules

_____

_____

_____

Choose interesting activities

_____

_____

_____

List rewards for good behavior

_____

_____

_____

List consequences for misbehavior

_____

_____

_____

Note any goals from the follow-up discussion

_____

_____

_____

worksheets

planned activities checklist

Situation: ....

Instructions: Whenever this situation happens record Yes, No or NA (Not Applicable) for each of the steps below.

	DAY						
STEPS TO FOLLOW	**STEPS COMPLETED?**						
1.							
2.							
3.							
4.							
5.							
6.							
NUMBER OF STEPS COMPLETED:							

worksheets

notes

notes

notes